Reading
for
Proficiency

A Test Preparation Program

Level B

GLOBE FEARON
Pearson Learning Group

Reviewers:

Bettye J. Birden
Language Arts Department Chairperson
Houston Independent School District
Houston, Texas

Sally Parker, M.A.
Language Arts Resource Teacher
Elk Grove Unified School District
Sacramento, California

Executive Editor: Jean Liccione
Project Editor: Kim Choi
Senior Editor: Lynn Kloss
Production Editor: Alan Dalgleish
Designer: Jennifer Visco
Composition: Phyllis Rosinsky

Acknowledgments:

Grateful acknowledgment is given to authors, publishers, and agents for permissions to reprint the following copyrighted material.

Page 19: "About Crows" by John Ciardi. Reprinted by permission of The Ciardi Family.

Pages 22–23: Excerpt from "The Guinea Pig" in *My Sister Eileen,* copyright 1938 and renewed 1966 by Ruth McKenney, reprinted by permission of Harcourt Brace & Company.

Pages 38–40: Excerpt from *Rain of Troubles.* Reprinted with the permission of Atheneum Books for Young Readers, an imprint of Simon & Schuster Children's Publishing Division from *Rain of Troubles* by Laurence Pringle. Copyright © 1988 Laurence Pringle.

Pages 52–53: "The Liberry" by Bel Kaufman originally appeared in *The New York Times,* July 31, 1976. Reprinted by permission of the author.

Page 53: "What the Library Means to Me" by Amy Tan. Copyright by Amy Tan. Used by permission of Amy Tan and the Sandra Dijkstra Literary Agency.

Pages 70–72: "The Trout" by Sean O'Faolain „ 1983 by Sean O'Faolain. First appeared in The Collected Stories of Sean O'Faolain published by Atlantic/Little Brown Books. Reprinted by permission of Curtis Brown, Ltd.

Pages 78–79: "The Old Block" by Anna Quindlen, *The New York Times,* May 17, 1992. Copyright 1992 by The New York Times Co. Reprinted by permission.

ISBN 0-835-94859-5
Printed in the United States of America
9 10 11 12   10 09 08 07

1-800-321-3106
www.pearsonlearning.com

CONTENTS

CONTENTS

INTRODUCTION
Succeeding on the Reading Test

Soon you'll be taking a reading test. So will many other students. As they prepare for a test, most students have three big questions on their minds:

1. What's going to be on the test?
2. How can this book help me succeed on the test?
3. How can I get a good score on the test?

The main purpose of this book is to answer these questions for you.

 BIG QUESTION 1: WHAT'S GOING TO BE ON THE TEST?
The reading test will have four different types of texts, or reading passages. Since each type of text is different, you'll need special skills and strategies to read each passage and answer the questions.

A. Different Kinds of Reading Passages on the Test
Here are the four types of reading passages you'll find on the test:

- **Narrative text** is writing that tells a story. Stories and novels are the most common narrative texts.

- **Informational text** is writing that mainly gives information about a topic. Your science and social studies textbooks are examples of informational text.

- **Persuasive text** is writing that tries to convince you to do something or think in a certain way. Editorials, letters to the editor, and advertisements are examples of persuasive text.

- **Everyday text** is the type of writing you see every day. Food labels, sets of directions, and lists of rules are examples of this text.

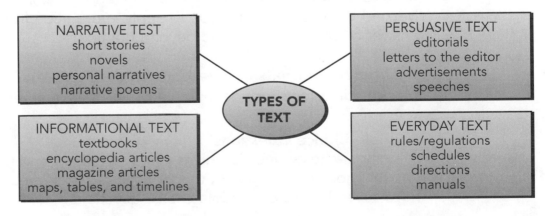

B. Different Levels of Questions on the Test

Each reading passage on the test is followed by multiple-choice questions. You can answer some of these questions by simply reading the lines of the text. To answer other questions, you'll need to read "between the lines" or even read "beyond the lines" of the actual passage.

Reading the Lines The answers to many questions are stated directly in the reading passage. All you need to do is read the lines carefully. For example, an informational passage might describe how four different species of wolves have been reintroduced into different regions of the United States in recent years. A multiple-choice question for this article might ask which species was reintroduced into New Mexico. By reading the lines carefully, you can find the correct answer.

Reading Between the Lines The answers to some questions are not stated directly in the text. These answers are only *implied* in the text. To figure out the answer yourself, you'll have to use details in the text as well as what you know from real life. For example, a question might ask you which statement best summarizes the message of a story. Since the author does not state the message directly in the text, you'll have to read between the lines. That means you'll think again about the characters, their actions, and the final outcome. From these details and what you know from your own experiences, you can decide which answer choice best states the message.

Reading Beyond the Lines A few questions may ask you to take a word or idea from a text and use it in another situation. For example, a persuasive editorial might accuse a school board of "robbing Peter to pay Paul" when it decided to buy sports equipment instead of library books. A question about this editorial might ask you to decide which of four different situations in the answer choices is also an example of "robbing Peter to pay Paul." These answer choices, however, would not have to do with the school board or related issues. In short, "reading beyond the lines" requires you to apply information from one text to answer questions that extend beyond the text.

C. Different Formats of Questions on the Test

Most reading tests include multiple-choice and open-ended questions.

Multiple-Choice Questions

A multiple-choice question gives you a statement and four possible answer choices. Only one of the four choices is correct. The test will have several types of multiple-choice questions.

- **Complete-Sentence Questions** This type of question is a complete sentence. Each answer choice is a complete sentence, too.

> What change happened to Denise at the end of the story?
>
> A. She became more self-assured and confident.
>
> B. Her grades in school improved markedly.
>
> C. She made several new friends among her classmates.
>
> D. She was embarrassed by her new status as class hero.

- **Sentence-Completion Questions** This type of question is not a complete sentence. Instead, you have to choose the answer that best completes the opening statement.

> This story is narrated by
>
> A. Danielle.
>
> B. another student in the biology class.
>
> C. the school principal.
>
> D. Danielle's biology teacher.

- **Special-Wording Questions** Some questions are worded in ways that require special attention. For example, they may ask you to choose the *best* or *most likely* answer. Or the question may ask you to choose the answer that is *not* something. For these questions, three of the answer choices would be correct if the word *not* was taken out of the question.

> Which of the following is NOT mentioned in the editorial as a reason for relocating the community center th the new mall
>
> A. The present community center building is too small.
>
> B. Most town residents want the center to be at the mall.
>
> C. The center has been offered free space at the mall.
>
> D. The old location has no convenient parking.

- **Vocabulary Questions** Vocabulary questions ask about the meanings of words in the passage. Usually, you will have to read between the lines and use context clues in the passage to figure out the meaning.

> From details in the passage, you can determine that asseverate means
>
> A. affirm.
>
> B. deny.
>
> C. marvel.
>
> D. imitate.

Open-Ended Questions

Open-ended questions ask you to write answers in your own words on special writing lines. The questions can be answered in many different ways, but usually they must be based on information in the reading passage. Open-ended questions are an opportunity to show how well you have read and understood a passage.

You will usually begin an open-ended answer with a statement of your main idea. The rest of the answer will be details and examples that support your main idea.

> **Would you like to have Ron as a friend? Explain your answer based on what you learned about him in the story.**
>
>   Based on Ron's behavior, I would probably not want to be his friend.
> He "borrowed" money from the class treasury and then lied about
> returning it. I would not trust him enough to become friends with him.
> I also thought the was mean, locking his kid brother out of the house
> while he was having a party.

 BIG QUESTION 2: HOW CAN THIS BOOK HELP ME SUCCEED ON THE TEST?

This book is organized and designed with you in mind. All of the features described below will help you do well on your reading test.

- **Chapter Openers** Each chapter opener gives you an overview of one of the types of reading found on tests. The openers also answer the questions you're most likely to ask about these texts. Finally, you'll be introduced to some typical questions taken from actual tests.

- **Lessons** The lessons in each chapter focus on the skills you will need on reading tests. Each lesson also includes some valuable test-taking tips. After answering the question in the first part of a lesson, you can check your own answer. The book explains each answer choice and why it's right or wrong. You can then practice the skills you learned in completing the second part of the lesson.

- **Chapter Tests** At the end of each chapter, you'll find a reading test. This test focuses on the type of text presented in the chapter. Here's a chance to work with all the skills you have learned in the chapter at once. The clock symbol on the test shows you how much time you have to answer the questions.

- **Practice Test** After you've worked through the four chapters, you can try the Practice Test. It has four parts—one for each type of text you've studied. The Practice Test is similar to the test you'll take.

- **Reading Comprehension Skills Mini-Lessons** Check out the nine mini-lessons at the back of the book. They review many of the important reading skills that will help you answer test questions.

- **Glossary** The last page of the book is a glossary. That's where to check the meaning of the special words and terms in this book.

 BIG QUESTION 3: HOW CAN I GET A GOOD SCORE ON THE TEST?
By completing this book, you'll take a giant step toward scoring high on your next reading test. It is also important to answer the following questions before and during the test. The more *Yes* answers you have, the more successful you'll be!

Answering Questions
✔ Did I read the question carefully?
✔ Did I read all of the possible answers?
✔ Did I eliminate the obvious wrong answers before guessing at the right one?

Managing Time
✔ Is there a clock to help me use my time well?
✔ Do I know how much time to give to each part of the test?
✔ Am I careful not to get bogged down on any one question?
✔ Am I working quickly and steadily?

Completing the Answer Sheet
✔ Am I sure I understand how to fill in answers?
✔ Did I fill in the oval that corresponds to my answer choice for each question?
✔ Did I fill in the oval darkly and completely?
✔ Did I fill in only one oval for each answer?
✔ Before changing an answer, did I completely erase the old answer?

Doing My Personal Best
✔ Did I get a good night's rest before the test?
✔ Did I wake up early and eat a good breakfast?
✔ Did I collect my thoughts and relax before the test?
✔ Do I have confidence in myself?

Every reading test will include some **narrative text**. These questions and answers will help you learn more about this important type of writing.

 What is a narrative text?
Any writing that tells a story is a narrative text.

 What types of reading materials are narrative texts?
Two of the most common genres, or types, of narrative text are short stories and novels. It may also take the form of autobiographies, biographies, personal narratives, and even narrative poems. Regardless of the form, a narrative text tells a story in a connected series of events.

 What are the major elements of narrative text?

- **Characters** are the people in a short story or novel. Each character has certain qualities, or **character traits**, that the reader discovers as the story unfolds. Characters also have **motivations** that cause them to act in a certain way. A motivation might be a feeling or a goal.

- The **plot** is the sequence of events that happens in a story or novel. Usually the plot involves one or more **conflicts**, or struggles, between two opposing forces. The **resolution** of the plot shows how the conflict is resolved, or cleared up.

- The **setting** is the **time** and **place** in which the action of a story takes place. Often, the setting affects the **mood**, or atmosphere, of the story.

- The **theme** of a story is the main idea or message that the author wants you to think about or learn.

- **Figures of speech** include the use of imaginative language that is not meant to be taken as literal truth. Some common figures of speech are **similes, metaphors, personification,** and **hyperbole**.

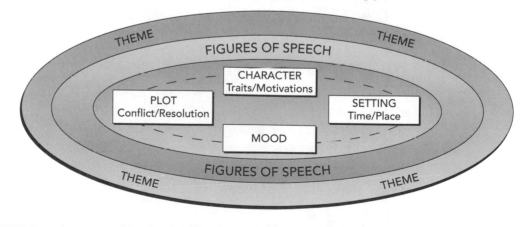

Test Questions About Narrative Text

Most test questions about narrative text focus on character, plot, setting, mood, theme, and figures of speech. Although questions take many different forms, certain types of questions are common. The questions below, which are taken from actual tests, will help you become familiar with the most common types of questions about narrative text.

Questions About Characters (Traits and Motivations)

- Which statement BEST describes Antonio?
- Which words BEST describe Tía Maria?
- Which doe Juan decide to return the money at the end of the story?
- What can you learn about Mr. Herrington from his dialogue?

Questions About Plot (Conflict and Resolution)

- What is Anita's main conflict at her new school?
- How did Jerry resolve the first conflict he faced at summer camp?
- Which conflict is never fully resolved in the story?
- How does Leon hope to end his family's feud with the Feuchtwangers?

Questions About Setting and Mood

- When does the action in this story take place?
- Where does the action in this story take place?
- Which words BEST describe the atmosphere of this story?
- How does news of the escape convicts affect the mood of the story?

Questions About Theme

- Which proverb of maxim BEST states the message of the story?
- What lesson does the author want readers to learn?
- Why do you think the author ended the story the way she did?

Questions About Figurative Language

- To describe the turtle's shell in stanza 2, the poet uses a _____.
- Which sentence fro the story includes an example of a metaphor?
- Why does the author use hyperbole to describe the sirens?
- The poet personifies the building by giving it which human feature?

The lessons in Chapter 1 will help you understand how to answer test questions about character, plot, setting, mood, theme, and figures of speech. You'll read some short story passages, poems, and other narrative texts and answer a few questions about each one. The questions will help you focus on these important elements of narrative text.

Character

A **character** is a person in a story or play. Each character has certain qualities, or **traits,** that the reader discovers as the events unfold. A character's words and actions usually show these traits. Sometimes an author states the character's traits directly. Another character in a story can also tell the reader what a character is like. **Motivation** is a feeling, idea, or goal that causes a character to act in a certain way.

Tips for Success

- Look for adjectives that tell what a character is like.
- Decide what a character's words or actions say about him or her.
- Notice how events cause a character to act during a story.

In this passage from *Anne of Green Gables* by L. M. Montgomery, the main character, an orphan named Anne, is driving to her new home in a horse and carriage. As you read, think about Anne's character traits.

She came out of her reverie with a deep sigh and looked at him with the dreamy gaze of a soul that had been wondering afar, star-led.

"Oh, Mr. Cuthbert," she whispered, "that place we came through—that white place—what was it?"

"Well now, you must mean the Avenue," said Matthew after a few moments' profound reflection. "It is a kind of pretty place."

"Pretty? Oh, *pretty* doesn't seem the right word to use. Nor beautiful, either. They don't go far enough. Oh, it was wonderful—wonderful. It's the first thing I ever saw that couldn't be improved upon by imagination . . . ."

". . . . But they shouldn't call that lovely place the Avenue. There is no meaning in a name like that. They should call it—let me see—the White Way of Delight. Isn't that a nice imaginative name? When I don't like the name of a place or a person I always imagine a new one and always think of them so. There was a girl at the asylum whose name was Hepzibah Jenkins, but I always imagined her as Rosalia DeVere. . . ."

1. Based on this passage, which statement BEST describes Anne?

   A. She is anxious to impress adults.

   B. She is unable to accept the ugliness that is part of reality.

   C. Her deep feelings for beauty and romance inspire her.

   D. She is very impractical and lives in a dream world.

1. Ⓐ Ⓑ Ⓒ Ⓓ

Mark your answer choice by filling in the oval.

Now check to see whether you chose the correct answer.

   A. The details in this passage do not suggest this about Anne.

   B. Although Anne is moved by beauty, readers don't know whether or not she can accept the ugly parts of reality.

   C. This is the correct answer. Anne is romantic and deeply moved by beauty.

   D. While Anne tends to be dreamy, readers don't know that she is impractical.

As you read this passage, think about the characters' traits and motivations.

When little Nephew Tatsuo came to live with us he liked to do everything the adults were doing in the nursery, and although his little mind did not know it, everything he did was opposite of adult conduct, unknowingly destructive and disturbing. So Uncle Hiroshi after witnessing several weeks of rampage said, "This has got to stop, this sawing the side of a barn and nailing the doors to see if it would open. But we must not whip him. We must not crush his curiosity by any means."

And when Nephew Tatsuo, who was seven and in high second grade, got used to the place and began coming out into the fields and pestering us with difficult questions as "What are the plants here for? What is water? Why are the bugs made for? What are the birds and why do the birds sing?" and so on, I said to Uncle Hiroshi, "We must do something about this. We cannot answer questions all the time and we cannot be correct all the time and so we will do

harm. But something must be done about this beyond a doubt."

"Let us take him in our hands," Uncle Hiroshi said.

So Hiroshi took little Nephew Tatsuo aside, and brought him out in the fields and showed him the many rows of pompons growing. "Do you know what these are?" Uncle Hiroshi said. "These things here?"

"Yes. Very valuable," Nephew Tatsuo said. "Plants."

"Do you know when these plants grow up and flower, we eat?" Uncle Hiroshi said.

Nephew Tatsuo nodded. "Yes," he said, "I knew that."

"All right. Uncle Hiroshi will give you six rows of pompons," Uncle Hiroshi said. "You own these six rows. You take care of them. Make them grow and flower like your uncles'."

—Toshio Mori, "The Six Rows of Pompons"

---

1. Ⓐ Ⓑ Ⓒ Ⓓ
2. Ⓐ Ⓑ Ⓒ Ⓓ

Mark the best answer for questions 1–2.

1. Which adjectives BEST describe Uncle Hiroshi?

   A. wise and patient

   B. old-fashioned and determined

   C. generous but misguided

   D. well-meaning but powerless

2. Why do you think Uncle Hiroshi gave Tatsuo the rows of pompons?

   A. He wants to punish Tatsuo for causing so much difficulty.

   B. He wants to help Tatsuo learn to appreciate the beauty of flowers.

   C. He wants Tatsuo to earn money to help support the family.

   D. He wants Tatsuo to become more mature and responsible.

Lesson 2 Plot

The series of events that make up a story is called the **plot**. The plot is "what happens" in the story and often centers on a conflict that a character faces. A **conflict** is a struggle between two or more opposing forces. The plot of a story also includes a **resolution** which shows how the conflict is resolved, or cleared up.

Tips for Success

- Pay attention to how each story event leads to the next event.
- Look for the main conflict a character faces.
- Focus on how the conflict is resolved.

Think about the conflict that Whirlwind, a Sioux grandmother, faces in this excerpt from *Buffalo Woman* **by Dorothy Johnson.**

Her back was toward the baby when she heard him shriek with glee. She turned instantly—and saw a dreadful thing. Between her and the baby was another kind of baby, an awkward little bear cub, the cub of the frightfully dangerous grizzly bear. The cub itself was harmless, but the old-woman bear, its mother, must be near, and she would protect her child.

Whirlwind did not even think of danger to herself. She ran to save her cub. She snatched up the baby on his cradleboard and threw him, with all her strength, above her head toward the level top of the cutbank.

At that moment the old-woman bear appeared. She snarled and came running, a shambling, awkward-looking run but very fast.

Whirlwind saw with horror the cradleboard with its precious burden sliding back down the cutbank. She had been too close when she threw the baby upward. The baby was screaming. Grandmother Whirlwind ran, picked up the cradleboard, ran back a few steps, and then threw hard again. This time the bundle stayed up there.

Whirlwind ran again toward the cutbank and climbed as fast as she could, digging into the dirt frantically with clutching fingers and digging toes.

1. What is Whirlwind's main conflict in the story?

   A. She and her grandchild may be attacked by a grizzly bear.

   B. She can't decide whether to save herself or her grandchild.

   C. She can't throw the baby up onto the cutbank to safety.

   D. She doesn't want the grizzly bear to see her.

Mark your answer choice by filling in the oval.

✔ **Now check to see whether you chose the correct answer.**

   A. This is the correct answer. Whirlwind and her grandchild are under attack.

   B. Whirlwind doesn't think twice about trying to save the baby first.

   C. On her second attempt, she does get the baby up onto the cutbank.

   D. The grizzly bear has already seen her and is rushing toward them.

This passage is about Shoots, Grandmother Whirlwind's young grandson. As you continue to read from *Buffalo Woman*, think about the main character's conflict and how it is resolved.

He saw a bundle fly through the air and slide down the cutbank. It happened too fast for him to see that it was the cradleboard with his baby brother. He heard fast movement in the weeds as Whirlwind ran back and threw the cradleboard again. He stood up, mouth open, just as she scrambled up the bank. With horror he saw the old-woman bear's claws **rake** her struggling legs.

With his heart in his mouth he did the best thing he could think of. He dropped his bow and grabbed the cub with both hands, so that it squalled with fear and pain. Then he threw it hard —past its mother.

Hearing her child cry, the woman bear whirled away from the cutbank to protect her cub. Shoots snatched up his bow; it was a good one, as strong as he could pull, and in a quiver on his shoulder he had six hunting arrows tipped with sharpened iron. At his waist he had a good steel knife.

But his enemy was better armed, with twenty immensely long, curved, sharp, death-dealing claws and a mouthful of long, sharp teeth, and she weighed more than five times as much as he did . . . .

He stood his ground and fired his arrows at her, fast but very carefully. . . . The woman bear yelled in pain and fury. She batted at the arrows deep in her flesh. She bit at them. But she kept coming.

Then Shoots did the last thing he could do, because it was too late to run. While the grizzly fought at the arrows, especially one that had gone into her left eye, he leaped on her back. With all his strength he sank his good steel knife into her throat . . . .

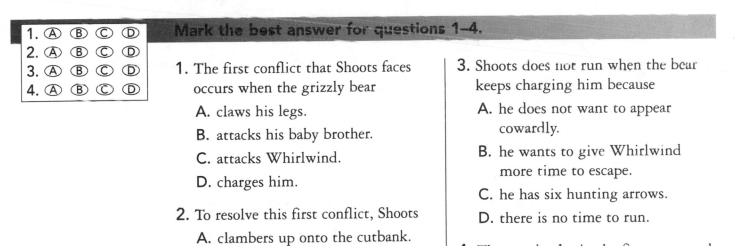

1. Ⓐ Ⓑ Ⓒ Ⓓ
2. Ⓐ Ⓑ Ⓒ Ⓓ
3. Ⓐ Ⓑ Ⓒ Ⓓ
4. Ⓐ Ⓑ Ⓒ Ⓓ

Mark the best answer for questions 1–4.

1. The first conflict that Shoots faces occurs when the grizzly bear
   A. claws his legs.
   B. attacks his baby brother.
   C. attacks Whirlwind.
   D. charges him.

2. To resolve this first conflict, Shoots
   A. clambers up onto the cutbank.
   B. throws the cub to distract its mother.
   C. runs to the village for help.
   D. shoots the bear in the eye.

3. Shoots does not run when the bear keeps charging him because
   A. he does not want to appear cowardly.
   B. he wants to give Whirlwind more time to escape.
   C. he has six hunting arrows.
   D. there is no time to run.

4. The word **rake** in the first paragraph means
   A. to gather or loosen with a tool.
   B. to search thoroughly.
   C. to glance over rapidly.
   D. to cut or scratch.

Lesson 3 Setting and Mood

The **setting** is the **time** and the **place** in which the action of a story takes place. Often, the author states where and when the story takes place. At other times, you have to use details to figure out the setting.

The setting can create a certain **mood** or atmosphere. A story set in a garden on a fine day could help create an upbeat mood, while an abandoned house on a stormy night might suggest a fearful mood.

Tips for Success

- Remember that the setting includes both the time and the place.
- Look for details that express the mood or atmosphere.
- Determine how the setting affects the characters or the events of the plot.

As you read the following excerpt from a story, think about the setting and how it affects the mood of the story.

At Santa Ysabel del Mar the season was at one of those moments when the air rests quiet over land and sea. The old breezes were gone; the new ones were not yet risen. The flowers in the mission garden opened wide; no wind came by day or night to shake the loose petals from their stems. Along the basking, silent, many-colored shore gathered and lingered the crisp odors of the mountains. The dust hung golden and motionless . . . and the Pacific lay like a floor of sapphire, whereon to walk beyond the setting sun into the East. One white sail shone there. Instead of an hour, it had been from dawn till afternoon in sight between the short headlands; and the Padre had hoped that it might be the ship his homesick heart awaited. But it had slowly passed. From an arch in his garden cloisters, he was now watching the last of it. Presently it was gone, and the great ocean lay empty.

—Owen Wister, "Padre Ignacio"

1. Which statement BEST describes the setting and mood of the passage?

   A. The setting, a beautiful beachfront garden in the present day, creates a mood of optimism and joy.

   B. The setting, a deserted beach on a winter day, suggests a mood of fear.

   C. The setting, a windless day at a Pacific coast mission some time ago, creates a sad mood of longing.

   D. The setting, a sailboat off the California coast in recent years, creates a mood of suspense.

1. Ⓐ Ⓑ Ⓒ Ⓓ   **Mark your answer choice by filling in the oval.**

✔ **Now check to see whether you chose the correct answer.**

   A. The mood is not optimistic and the time does not seem to be the present.

   B. Nothing suggests that it is winter, and the mood is sad but not fearful.

   C. This is the correct answer. The sailing ship and the Padre suggest the story is not set in the present. The weather and the Padre's homesickness create a sense of longing.

   D. Although a sailing ship is mentioned, the action is not set on one.

Read these opening paragraphs of the short story "To Build a Fire" by Jack London. As you read, pay attention to the story details.

Day had broken cold and gray, exceedingly cold and gray, when the man turned aside from the main Yukon trail and climbed the high earth bank, where a dim and little-traveled trail led eastward through the fat spruce timberland. It was a steep bank, and he paused for breath at the top, excusing the act to himself by looking at his watch. It was nine o'clock. There was no sun or hint of sun, though there was not a cloud in the sky. It was a clear day, and yet there seemed an intangible pall over the face of things, a subtle gloom that made the day dark, and that was due to the absence of sun. This fact did not worry the man. He was used to the lack of sun. It had been days since he had seen the sun. . . .

But all this—the mysterious, far-reaching hairline trail, the absence of sun from the sky, the tremendous cold, and the strangeness and weirdness of it all—made no impression on the man. It was not because he was long used to it. He was a newcomer in the land, a *chechaquo,* and this was his first winter. The trouble with him was that he was without imagination. He was quick and alert in the things of life, but only in the things, and not in the significances. Fifty degrees below zero meant eighty-odd degrees of frost. Such fact impressed him as being cold and uncomfortable, and that was all. It did not lead him to meditate upon his frailty as a creature of temperature, and upon man's frailty in general . . . . Fifty degrees below zero stood for a bite of frost that hurt and that must be guarded against by the use of mittens, ear flaps, warm moccasins, and thick socks. . . .

Mark the best answer for questions 1–3.

1. Ⓐ Ⓑ Ⓒ Ⓓ
2. Ⓐ Ⓑ Ⓒ Ⓓ
3. Ⓐ Ⓑ Ⓒ Ⓓ

1. The setting in this story is
   A. in a small cabin.
   B. along the banks of a river.
   C. out on the frozen sea ice.
   D. on a trail through a forest.

2. The sun is not shining because the story is set
   A. at nighttime.
   B. during a snowstorm.
   C. in the far north.
   D. on a cloudy day.

3. In general, the details about the setting create what type of mood?
   A. upbeat
   B. relaxed
   C. gloomy
   D. frustrated

4. Based on the man's attitude toward the setting, predict what might happen.

_____

_____

_____

Lesson 4 Theme

The **theme** is the message or the main idea that the author wants you to get from the writing. Usually, an author doesn't state the theme directly. Instead, the theme becomes apparent as the characters experience events. By paying close attention to the events and outcome, you should be able to determine the theme.

Tips for Success
- Focus on the message the author wants to get across.
- Decide which answer choice best sums up the main idea of the story.

As you read this narrative from *The Autobiography of Benjamin Franklin*, think about the theme that the author presents.

I believe I have omitted mentioning that, in my first voyage from Boston, being becalmed off Block Island, our people set about catching cod, and hauled up a great many. Hitherto I had stuck to my resolution of not eating animal food, and on this occasion I considered . . . the taking of fish as a kind of unprovoked murder, since none of them had, or ever could do us any injury that might justify the slaughter. All this seemed very reasonable. But I had formerly been a great lover of fish, and, when this came hot out of the frying-pan, it smelled admirably well. I balanced some time between principle and inclination, till I recollected that, when the fish were opened, I saw smaller fish taken out of their stomachs; then thought I, "If you eat one another, I don't see why we mayn't eat you." So I dined upon cod very heartily, and continued to eat with other people, returning only now and then occasionally to a vegetable diet.

1. What message can you infer from this story?

A. Most vegetarians aren't really serious about not eating meat.

B. When you are tempted to do something, you can often find a reason to do it.

C. In the world of nature, the big and the powerful prey upon the small and the weak.

D. When caught in a serious situation, you must sometimes compromise your values.

1. Ⓐ Ⓑ Ⓒ Ⓓ

Mark your answer choice by filling in the oval.

✔ **Now check to see whether you chose the correct answer.**

A. The passage is only about Benjamin Franklin, not about vegetarians in general.

B. This is the correct answer. Franklin shows how easily temptation caused him to change his mind.

C. While Franklin observes that big fish ate little fish, this is not the main idea he wishes to express.

D. Franklin was not really in a serious situation and he was not forced to compromise.

As you read these poems, think about their themes.

About Crows

The old crow is getting slow.
    The young crow is not.
Of what the young crow does not know
    The old crow knows a lot.

At knowing things the old crow
    Is still the young crow's master.
What does the slow old crow not know?
    How to go faster.

The young crow flies above, below,
    And rings around the slow old crow.
What does the fast young crow not know?
    Where to go.

                    —John Ciardi

XXIV

I saw a man pursuing the horizon;
Round and round they sped.
I was **disturbed** at this;
I accosted the man.
"It is futile," I said,
"You can never—"

"You lie," he cried,
And ran on.

                    —Stephen Crane

---

1. Ⓐ Ⓑ Ⓒ Ⓓ
2. Ⓐ Ⓑ Ⓒ Ⓓ
3. Ⓐ Ⓑ Ⓒ Ⓓ

Mark the best answer for questions 1–2.

1. What is the theme of the poem "About Crows"?

   A. The natural slowing down that comes with age frustrates the young.

   B. Don't expend too much energy if you don't know where you're going.

   C. The wisdom of experience is more important than youthful enthusiasm.

   D. The old envy the young.

2. The theme of the poem by Stephen Crane might be:

   A. You should never ignore helpful advice.

   B. There is more than one way to look at a situation.

   C. Achieving our goals requires extraordinary energy.

   D. You can usually help others by giving good advice.

3. The meaning of **disturbed** in line 3 of the poem by Stephen Crane is

   A. made worried, nervous, or upset.

   B. broke up the quiet or calm of a place.

   C. mixed up or put into disorder.

   D. broke in on or interrupted.

4. Read the Stephen Crane poem again. How would you describe its theme?

_____

_____

_____

Lesson 5 Figures of Speech

Writers use **figures of speech** to create imaginative descriptions.

- A **simile** is a figure of speech that makes a comparison between two things using the words *like* or *as*.

  The sunbaked mountains slump down to the sea like tired old dinosaurs.

- A **metaphor** is a figure of speech that makes a comparison by stating that one thing *is* another.

  The houses of the fishing village are whitewashed shoeboxes, scattered along the road.

- **Personification** gives human traits or abilities to an animal or object.

  By January, the village had crawled beneath its quilt of snow and fallen fast asleep.

- **Hyperbole** creates a striking image by exaggerating something.

  The bronco bucked so hard that I was in the air all afternoon.

Tips for Success

- Figures of speech point out unexpected connections.
- Remember that a figure of speech is not literally true. It helps you see things in a new way.

Read this poem, paying attention to the figures of speech.

The Eagle

He clasps the crag with crooked hands;
Close to the sun in lonely lands,
Ring'd with the azure world, he stands.

The wrinkled sea beneath him crawls;
He watches from his mountain walls,
And like a thunderbolt he falls.

—Alfred, Lord Tennyson

1. In the last line of the poem, what figure of speech does the poet use?
   A. personification
   B. metaphor
   C. simile
   D. hyberbole

1. Ⓐ Ⓑ Ⓒ Ⓓ   **Mark your answer choice by filling in the oval.**

✔ **Now check to see whether you chose the correct answer.**

   A. The poet does not give the eagle any human traits in the last line.

   B. The poet does not say the bird is a thunderbolt.

   C. This is the correct answer. The poet uses the word *like* to compare the eagle to a thunderbolt. This is a simile.

   D. The poet is not really using wild exaggeration here.

As you read these passages, look for figures of speech.

They are the only ones who understand me. I am the only one who understands them. Four skinny trees with skinny necks and pointy elbows like mine. Four who do not belong here but are here . . . .

Their strength is secret. They send ferocious roots beneath the ground. They grow up and they grow down and grab the earth between their hairy toes and bite the sky with violent teeth and never quit their anger. This is how they keep.

—Sandra Cisneros,
"Four Skinny Trees"

There is a smell of burning in small towns in afternoon, and men with buckles on their arms are raking leaves in yards as boys come by with straps slung back across their shoulders. The oak leaves, big and brown, are bedded deep in yard and gutter: they make deep wadings to the knee for children in the streets. The fire will snap and crackle like a whip, sharp acrid smoke will sting the eyes, in mown fields the little vipers of the flame eat past the black coarse edges of burned stubble like a line of locusts.

—Thomas Wolfe,
Of Time and the River

| 1. Ⓐ Ⓑ Ⓒ Ⓓ |
| 2. Ⓐ Ⓑ Ⓒ Ⓓ |
| 3. Ⓐ Ⓑ Ⓒ Ⓓ |
| 4. Ⓐ Ⓑ Ⓒ Ⓓ |

Mark the best answer for questions 1–4.

1. What type of figure of speech does Sandra Cisneros use?

   A. similes

   B. metaphors

   C. personification

   D. hyperbole

2. To what does Cisneros compare the trees' roots?

   A. fingers

   B. earth

   C. teeth

   D. toes

3. When he describes the crackle of the fire as the sound of a whip, Thomas Wolfe uses

   A. a simile.

   B. a metaphor.

   C. personification.

   D. hyperbole.

4. In describing the flame as vipers, Thomas Wolfe uses

   A. a metaphor.

   B. a simile.

   C. personification.

   D. hyperbole.

5. Identify two specific instances of figures of speech in Sandra Cisneros's description of the trees. Explain how you know they are figures of speech.

_____

_____

_____

In these pages, you can use the skills you have practiced in this chapter. Read this passage from the novel *My Sister Eileen* by Ruth McKenney and answer the questions. Mark your answer choices by filling in the ovals.

Lifesaving Course

1. From the very beginning of that awful lifesaving course I took the last season I went to girls' camp, I was a marked woman. The rest of the embryo lifesavers were little, slender maidens, but I am a peasant type, and I was monstrously big for my fourteen years. I approximated, in poundage anyway, the theoretical adult we energetic young lifesavers were scheduled to rescue, and so I was, for the teacher's purpose, the perfect guinea pig.

2. The first few days of the course were unpleasant for me, but not terribly dangerous. The elementary lifesaving hold, in case you haven't seen some hapless victim being rescued by our brave beach guardians, is a snakelike arrangement for supporting the drowning citizen with one hand while you paddle him in to shore with the other. You are supposed to wrap your arm around his neck and shoulders, and keep his head well above water by resting it on your collarbone.

3. This is all very well in theory, of course, but the trick that none of Miss Folgil's little pupils could master was keeping the victim's nose and mouth above the waterline. Time and again I was held in a viselike grip by one of the earnest students with my whole face an inch or two under the billowing waves.

4. "No, no, Betsy," Miss Folgil would scream through her megaphone, as I felt the water rush into my lungs. "No, no, you must keep the head a little higher." At this point I would begin to kick and struggle, and generally the pupil would have to let go while I came up for air. Miss Folgil was always very stern with me.

5. "Ruth," she would shriek from her boat, "I insist! You must allow Betsy to tow you all the way in. We come to Struggling in Lesson Six."

6. This was but the mere beginning, however. A few lessons later we came to the section of the course where we learned how to undress underwater in forty seconds. Perhaps I should say we came to the point where the *rest* of the pupils learned how to get rid of shoes and such while holding their breaths. I never did.

7. There was quite a little ceremony connected with this part of the course. Miss Folgil, and some lucky creature named as timekeeper and armed with a stopwatch, rowed the prospective victim out to deep water. The pupil, dressed in high, laced tennis shoes, long stockings, heavy bloomers, and a middy blouse, then stood poised at the end of the boat. When the timekeeper yelled "Go!" the future boon to mankind dived into the water and, while holding her breath under the surface, unlaced her shoes and stripped down to her bathing suit. Miss Folgil never explained what connection, if any, this curious rite had with saving human lives.

8. I had no middy of my own, so I borrowed one of my sister's. My sister was a slender little thing and I was, as I said, robust, which puts it politely. Eileen had some trouble wedging me into that middy, and once in it I looked like a stuffed sausage. It never occurred to me how hard it was going to be to get that middy off, especially when it was wet and slippery.

9. As we rowed out for my ordeal by undressing, Miss Folgil was snappish and bored.

10. "Hurry up," she said, looking irritated. "Let's get this over with quick. I don't think you're ready to pass the test anyway."

11. I was good and mad when I jumped off the boat, and determined to make good and show that old Miss Folgil, whom I was beginning to dislike thoroughly. As soon as I was underwater, I got my shoes off, and I had no trouble with the bloomers or stockings. I was just beginning to run out of breath when I held up my arms and started to pull off the middy.

12. Now, the middy, in the event you don't understand the principle of this girl-child garment, is made with a small head opening, long sleeves, and no front opening. You pull it on and off over your head. You do if you are lucky, that is. I got the middy just past my neck so that my face was covered with heavy linen cloth, when it stuck.

13. I pulled frantically and my lungs started to burst. Finally I thought the heck with the test, the heck with saving other people's lives, anyway. I came to the surface, a curious sight, my head enfolded in a water-soaked middy blouse. I made a brief sound, a desperate glub-glub, a call for help. My arms were stuck in the middy and I couldn't swim. I went down. I breathed in large quantities of water and linen cloth.

14. I came up again, making final frantic appeals. Four feet away sat a professional lifesaver, paying absolutely no attention to somebody drowning right under her nose. I went down again, struggling with last panic-stricken feverishness, fighting water and a middy blouse for my life. At this point the timekeeper pointed out to Miss Folgil that I had been under water for eighty-five seconds, which was quite a time for anybody. Miss Folgil was very annoyed, as she hated to get her bathing suit wet, but a thoughtful teacher, she picked up her megaphone, shouted to the rest of the class on the beach to watch, and dived in after me.

15. If I say so myself, I gave her quite a time rescuing me. I presented a new and different problem and probably am written up in textbooks now under the heading "What to Do When the Victim Is Entangled in a Tight Middy Blouse." Miss Folgil finally towed my still-breathing body over to the boat, reached for her bowie knife, which she carried on a ring with her whistle, and cut Eileen's middy straight up the front. Then she towed me with Hold No. 2 right in to shore and delivered me up to the class for artificial respiration. I will never forgive the Red Cross for that terrible trip through the water, when I might have been hoisted into the boat and rowed in except for Miss Folgil's overdeveloped sense of drama and **pedagogy**.

1. Ⓐ Ⓑ Ⓒ Ⓓ
2. Ⓐ Ⓑ Ⓒ Ⓓ
3. Ⓐ Ⓑ Ⓒ Ⓓ
4. Ⓐ Ⓑ Ⓒ Ⓓ
5. Ⓐ Ⓑ Ⓒ Ⓓ
6. Ⓐ Ⓑ Ⓒ Ⓓ
7. Ⓐ Ⓑ Ⓒ Ⓓ
8. Ⓐ Ⓑ Ⓒ Ⓓ

CHARACTER

1. Ruth's character could be described as
   A. timid and fearful.
   B. witty and self-aware.
   C. outgoing and boastful.
   D. witty and boastful.

FIGURES OF SPEECH

2. In the first paragraph, the author says she was "the perfect guinea pig." This is an example of
   A. a simile.
   B. a metaphor.
   C. personification.
   D. hyperbole.

CHARACTER

3. In general, what does Miss Folgil's manner of speech tell you about her?
   A. She doesn't know very much about lifesaving.
   B. She is genuinely fond of all the campers in her group.
   C. She values rules above all.
   D. She is happy-go-lucky and somewhat illogical.

PLOT

4. In paragraph 1, a major source of conflict for the narrator of the story is that
   A. she didn't know how to swim.
   B. she was older than the other girls at camp.
   C. she could not master the elementary lifesaving hold.
   D. she thinks she is large for her age.

SETTING

5. Most of the action in the story seems to take place in
   A. a swimming pool.
   B. a pond.
   C. a lake.
   D. a river.

SETTING

6. Based on the description in pagragraph 7 of what the girls wore in the water, you can infer that this story is MOST LIKELY set in
   A. the 1930s.
   B. the 1960s.
   C. the 1980s.
   D. the present day.

FIGURES OF SPEECH

7. In paragraph 7, Ruth McKenney describes a girl in the class as a "future boon to mankind." This is an example of
   A. a simile.
   B. a metaphor.
   C. personification.
   D. hyperbole.

FIGURES OF SPEECH

8. In paragraph 8, after putting on Eileen's middy, the author likens herself to a "stuffed sausage." This is an example of
   A. a simile.
   B. a metaphor.
   C. personification.
   D. hyperbole.

PLOT

9. Ruth's major conflict in the story becomes more serious than it needs to be because

    A. she doesn't know the elementary lifesaving hold.

    B. the timekeeper plays a trick on her.

    C. Miss Folgil isn't paying much attention to Ruth's situation.

    D. she is not supposed to struggle during the rescue.

MOOD

10. What word BEST describes the mood in paragraphs 13–15?

    A. upbeat

    B. mysterious

    C. suspenseful

    D. peaceful

CHARACTER

11. At the end of the story, Ruth seems to feel

    A. grateful that Miss Folgil has rescued her.

    B. embarrassed that the other girls must perform artificial respiration on her.

    C. annoyed that Miss Folgil has cut up and destroyed her sister's middy.

    D. resentful that Miss Folgil did not come to her rescue sooner.

VOCABULARY

12. The final word in paragraph 15, **pedagogy**, means

    A. fair play.

    B. teaching.

    C. difficulty.

    D. concern.

PLOT

13. The major conflict in the story is resolved when the narrator

    A. finds a way to get out of the middy blouse.

    B. is rescued by Miss Folgil.

    C. responds to artificial respiration.

    D. manages to swim to shore behind the boat.

THEME

14. Which message does the author seem to imply in this narrative?

    A. A mark of maturity is knowing when not to attempt difficult tasks.

    B. To get along, you have to go along.

    C. Learning to get along with teachers can be difficult.

    D. Fate sometimes seems to single us out for unpleasant experiences.

9. Ⓐ	Ⓑ	Ⓒ	Ⓓ
10. Ⓐ	Ⓑ	Ⓒ	Ⓓ
11. Ⓐ	Ⓑ	Ⓒ	Ⓓ
12. Ⓐ	Ⓑ	Ⓒ	Ⓓ
13. Ⓐ	Ⓑ	Ⓒ	Ⓓ
14. Ⓐ	Ⓑ	Ⓒ	Ⓓ

15. In this narrative, the author uses words and phrases to express the dark humor of her experiences in the lifesaving course. Choose three words or phrases from the story, and tell why you think each is funny.

_____

_____

_____

CHAPTER 2

Informational Text

A great deal of your education in school centers around informational text. Since this type of text is so important, reading tests check your ability to read and understand informational text.

 What is an informational text?
Anything that was written mainly to explain or give information about a topic is an informational text.

 What types of reading materials are informational texts?
The informational texts you're probably most familiar with are social studies and science textbooks. The articles in encyclopedias and other reference books are also informational text. Most books in the nonfiction section of the library are usually informational text. The news and feature articles in newspapers and magazines also give information.

 What are the major elements of an informational text?

- The **central purpose** is the focus of an informational text. It's what the author most wants you to learn.

- A **major idea** is the important point made in a section of informational text. Sometimes, it is called the **main idea**. The **supporting details** develop and explain the major or main ideas.

- **Maps, tables,** and **timelines** are **visual aids** that organize a great deal of information in an easy-to-use form.

- An **index** at the end of a book is an alphabetical list of topics in the book and the pages on which they are mentioned.

- A set of encyclopedias often has a book-length **encyclopedia index** that lists all the articles in the complete set. A **computer catalog** in the library provides additional sources of information.

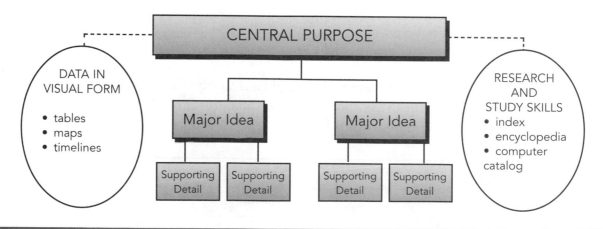

Test Questions About Informational Text

Most test questions about informational text focus on central purpose, major ideas, and supporting details. Often the tests include questions about maps, tables, or other visual aids in the text. The test may also ask questions about an index or library computer catalog. The questions below come from actual tests and show the most common types of questions that are asked about informational text.

Questions About Central Purpose

- What is the central purpose of this passage?
- What did the Author hope to accomplish by writing this selection?
- Choose the statement that is MOST important.

Questions About Major Ideas

- Which sentence BEST states the major idea of paragraphs 3–5?
- What is the main reason for the decline in the union membership?
- Why did the Soviet Union agree to remove its missiles from Cuba?
- In what way did the horses change the lifestyle of the Sioux?

Questions About Supporting Details

- How long did it take for Marco Polo to journey to China?
- Which silent screen actor was able to become a star in the "talkies"?
- Which is NOT listed as a drawback of water-cooled engines?
- Why are the camel's long legs a good desert adaptation?

Questions About Maps, Tables and Timelines

- According to the table, which city has the highest pollution level?
- According to the map, how long is the Suez Canal?
- According to the timeline, how long after the electric trolley was introduced did the first subway open?

Questions About Indexes and the Computer Catalog

- Which pages tell about the causes of the Boxer Rebellion?
- Which index topic would provide information on how wolves hunt?
- Which entry would you use to find information on the first computer?

The lessons in Chapter 2 will help you understand how to answer test questions about central purpose, major ideas, and supporting details in informational text. You'll read some short informational passages and answer a few questions. The upcoming lessons will also help you work with visual aids, indexes, and the computer catalog. The questions will help you focus on the important elements of informational text.

Central Purpose

Reading tests always include questions about the **central purpose** of an informational article. The central purpose is the focus of an informational text. This is what the author most wants you to learn. The central purpose of a news story about manatees in Florida, for example, might be to explain why they are endangered by motorboats.

To find the central purpose, think about all the different facts and ideas in an informational article. Usually, they work together to present the central purpose.

Tips for Success

- Ask yourself what the author most wants you to learn.
- Remember that a selection may contain many true statements that are not the central purpose.
- The central purpose is likely to be a general statement concerning the entire selection.

Read this passage about ants. Think about what the author most wants you to learn.

They go to war, often marching in columns and attacking in unison. They keep cattle in the form of smaller insects that give off honeydew, milk them regularly, and, in some cases, even build barns to shelter them. Some ants plant fungus gardens and gather crops like farmers. Others harvest grain and store it in granaries. Still others have servants and slaves to wait on them. Many ants keep pets in their homes. In fact, it is said that the ants have domesticated more different kinds of creatures than man has!

Sometimes, tropical ants live in great cities that contain half a million inhabitants. Their nests have been known to occupy as much as three hundred cubic yards of earth. Finally, like man and unlike most insects, ants live for years. Workers have a life span up to seven years and queens have been known to live eighteen years. The same underground cities are sometimes occupied for half a century, one generation of ants "inheriting real estate" from the generation before.

—Edwin Way Teale, *The Junior Book of Ants*

1. The central purpose of this passage is

   A. to show that ants are amazing insects.

   B. to explain that ants have a variety of food supplies.

   C. to suggest that ants resemble humans in a variety of ways.

   D. to suggest that we can learn about human society by studying ants.

1. Ⓐ Ⓑ Ⓒ Ⓓ   **Mark your answer choice by filling in the oval.**

✓ **Now check to see whether you chose the correct answer.**

   A. Ants are indeed amazing, but this isn't the central purpose of the piece.

   B. This is true, but it's not the main focus of the text.

   C. This is the correct answer. All the examples in the passage work to express this central purpose.

   D. The author may imply this, but it's not the main purpose of the article.

In this passage from *Aku-Aku*, Thor Heyerdahl describes gigantic statues he saw at Rano Raraku, a volcanic mountain on Easter Island in the Pacific Ocean. As you read, think about the central purpose.

. . . And in the midst of the mountain's gaping wound lie more than a hundred and fifty gigantic stone men, in all stages from the just begun to the just completed. At the foot of the mountain stand finished stone men side by side like a supernatural army.

. . . Dismounting from your horse in the shadow of a great block of stone, you see that the block has features on its underside: it is the head of a fallen giant. All twenty-three of our expedition could creep under it and find shelter in a rainstorm. On going up to the foremost figures, which are buried in the earth up to their chests, you are shocked to find that you cannot even reach up to the colossi's chins. And if you try to climb onto those which lie flat on their backs, you feel a regular **Lilliputian** because often you have the greatest difficulty even in getting up onto their stomachs. And once up on a **prostrate** Goliath you can walk about freely on his chest and stomach, or stretch yourself out on his nose, which often is as long as an ordinary bed. Thirty feet is no uncommon height for these figures. The largest, which lay unfinished and aslant on the side of the volcano, was sixty-nine feet long, so that, counting a story as ten feet, this stone man was as tall as a seven-story building.

1. Ⓐ Ⓑ Ⓒ Ⓓ
2. Ⓐ Ⓑ Ⓒ Ⓓ
3. Ⓐ Ⓑ Ⓒ Ⓓ

Mark the best answer for questions 1–3.

1. The author's central purpose in this passage is:
   A. to tell that the statues at the site are incomplete or lying on their sides.
   B. to show that the statues are buried up to their chests in earth.
   C. to explain that the statues range in size from thirty to almost seventy feet long.
   D. to show that the statues make humans feel tiny.

2. You can infer that **Lilliputians** are
   A. undersized people.
   B. stone carvers.
   C. vacationers or travelers
   D. members of an ancient tribe.

3. The clues in the text suggest that **prostrate** means
   A. made of stone.
   B. broken into pieces.
   C. lying flat.
   D. unfinished.

4. Write two questions you would like to ask Thor Heyerdahl about these statues.

_____

_____

_____

Major Idea and Supporting Details

A **major idea** is the most important idea in a paragraph or a group of paragraphs in a longer informational text. Sometimes an author states a major idea directly. Sometimes you have to figure it out from the details. To determine the major idea, ask yourself what the passage is about. Often, the major idea is a general statement that sums up the passage. **Supporting details** are the details in a passage that support, or tell more about, the major idea. These details are often facts, examples, or quotations.

Tips for Success

- Determine the most important point of a selection.
- Make sure you know what the major idea is before deciding whether a detail supports it.

As you read this passage from *The Sea Around Us* by Rachel Carson, look for the major idea and supporting details.

The sea transforms climate. And how completely it does so is strikingly seen in the differences between the Arctic and the Antarctic.

The Arctic is a sea almost closed in by land; the Antarctic is a continent surrounded by ocean. The ice-covered Antarctic is in the grip of high winds that blow outward from the land. They ward off any warming influence that might otherwise come to the continent from the sea. So the Antarctic is a bitterly cold land. Here and there over the snow is the red dust of very small and simple plant cells. Mosses hide from the wind in the valleys and crevices. But of the higher plants only a few skimpy strands of grasses have managed to find a foothold. . . .

Contrast with this the summers of the Arctic! Its flat, treeless plains are bright with many-colored flowers. Everywhere except on the Greenland icecap and some arctic islands, summer is warm enough for plants to grow. They pack a year's growth into the short, warm arctic summer. The limit of plant life toward the poles is set not by latitude, but by the sea. For the influence of the warm Atlantic is borne far up into the Arctic, making it in climate as well as geography a world apart from the Antarctic.

1. Which statement BEST describes the major idea of this passage?

   A. The sea transforms climate.

   B. The Antarctic is a continent surrounded by ocean.

   C. The animals of the Antarctic are birds, a wingless mosquito, and flies.

   D. The Greenland icecap and some arctic islands are not warm enough in summer for plants to grow.

1. Ⓐ Ⓑ Ⓒ Ⓓ **Mark your answer choice by filling in the oval.**

✓ **Now check to see whether you chose the correct answer.**

   A. This is the correct answer. It states the major idea of the passage.

   B. This statement applies only to the Antarctic.

   C. This statement is a detail that supports the major idea.

   D. This statement is another example of a supporting detail.

As you read this passage from *The Amazing Universe* by astronomer Herbert Friedman, think about its major idea and supporting details.

To begin a description of our amazing universe, we must try to appreciate its vast scale. "Try" is the right word, for astronomical distances are so great that it is extremely difficult—with our everyday, human concepts of time and space—to sense them at all. Because of the immensities involved, astronomers find a convenient measure in the speed of light: 186,282 miles a second.

A ray of light travels from moon to earth in slightly more than a second, so the earth-moon distance—240,000 miles—can be expressed as about 1.3 light-seconds. The 93 million miles from sun to earth is the equivalent of 8.3 light-minutes. A light-year, the astronomical measure commonly used, is about *six trillion* miles.

Since today's rockets never achieve more than a small fraction of the speed of light, space travel requires about three days to the moon, two years to Jupiter, and 15 years to Pluto. To reach the nearest star, Alpha Centauri, at a distance of 4.3 light-years, would take nearly 100,000 years!

Stand out of doors in the country on a clear night and look up: Without a magnifying lens you can see several thousand stars. A pair of binoculars will bring into view perhaps 50,000. If you have a two-inch telescope, the number leaps to several hundred thousand. The current estimate is that our galaxy, the Milky Way, contains about 200 billion stars, many of them in clusters of hundreds of thousands.

1. Ⓐ Ⓑ Ⓒ Ⓓ
2. Ⓐ Ⓑ Ⓒ Ⓓ

Mark the best answer for questions 1–2.

1. What is the major idea of this passage?
   A. Our galaxy contains hundreds of billions of stars.
   B. The size of the universe makes space travel impractical.
   C. Most of the galaxy is not visible, even to astronomers with telescopes.
   D. The vast size of our universe is almost impossible to grasp.

2. Which of these details BEST supports the major idea of the passage?
   A. A light-year is about six trillion miles.
   B. Our galaxy contains about 200 billion stars.
   C. A ray of light travels from moon to earth in just over a second.
   D. The galaxy takes the form of a disk with a bulge at the center.

3. Write a sentence that states the main idea of the last paragraph.

_____

_____

_____

Lesson 3 Data in Visual Form

Many informational texts include **timelines**, **tables**, and **maps**. These visual aids, which appear on many reading tests, contain a great deal of information that is clearly organized and easy to read. By using these visuals, you can find information quickly.

USING A TIMELINE

A **timeline** divides a given period of time into equal segments. The dates of significant events that occurred during the period are shown above and below the timeline. Timelines put history in perspective. In addition to listing the order of events, they show at a glance how much time elapsed between various events.

Tips for Success

- Always read the titles of timelines, tables, and maps.
- Look carefully at the labels that appear on the rows and columns of tables.
- Use a map's legend and scale to help you answer questions.
- Read "between the lines" of visual aids to draw conclusions.

Here is a timeline showing the history of the early people of the Americas.

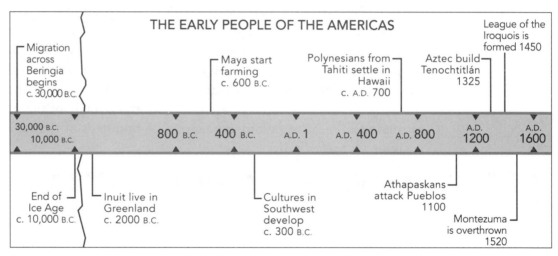

1. What was the next event to occur after the cultures in the Southwest developed?

   A. The Athapaskans attacked the Pueblos.

   B. The Maya started farming.

   C. The League of the Iroquois was formed.

   D. The Polynesians from Tahiti settled in Hawaii.

1. Ⓐ Ⓑ Ⓒ Ⓓ **Mark your answer choice by filling in the oval.**

✔ **Now check to see whether you chose the correct answer.**

   A. Check the timeline again. Be sure to look at events above and below the timeline.

   B. Check the timeline again.

   C. Check the timeline again.

   D. This is the correct answer. The timeline shows this sequence of events.

Test Practice

Look back at the timeline on page 32 to answer questions 1–2.

Look back at the timeline on page 32 to answer questions 1–2.

1. Ⓐ Ⓑ Ⓒ Ⓓ
2. Ⓐ Ⓑ Ⓒ Ⓓ

1. How long had the Inuit been in Greenland when the cultures of the Southwest began to develop?

   A. 300 years

   B. 800 years

   C. 1700 years

   D. 2000 years

2. Which event occurred first?

   A. The Iroquois form their League.

   B. The Athapascans attack the Pueblos.

   C. Montezuma is overthrown.

   D. Polynesians from Tahiti settle in Hawaii.

USING A TABLE

A **table** is an arrangement of facts in rows and columns. Each row and column has a **label**. Read down the column and across the rows to find the information you need.

Here is a table from a science textbook.

GEOLOGIC TIME SCALE

Time	Era	Period	Epoch	Years Before Present
Phanerozoic	Cenozoic	Quaternary	Recent	11,000
			Pleistocene	1.6 million
		Tertiary	Pliocene	5 million
			Miocene	24 million
			Oligocene	37 million
			Eocene	58 million
			Paleocene	66 million
	Mesozoic	Cretaceous		130 million
		Jurassic		190 million
		Triassic		249 million
	Paleozoic	Permian		290 million
		Carboniferous		350 million
		Devonian		395 million
		Silurian		425 million
		Ordovician		500 million
		Cambrian		570 million
Precambrian	Proterozoic			2,500 million
	Archean			4,600 million

Use the table to answer questions 3–4.

3. Ⓐ Ⓑ Ⓒ Ⓓ
4. Ⓐ Ⓑ Ⓒ Ⓓ

3. About how many years before the present was the Paleocene Epoch?

   A. 37 million

   B. 58 million

   C. 66 million

   D. 130 million

4. Fossils thought to be 130 million years old date from

   A. the Cenozoic Era.

   B. the Cretaceous Period.

   C. the Paleocene Epoch.

   D. Precambrian Time.

USING A MAP

A **map** is a visual representation of a place. To find distances on a map, use the **scale**. To find out about specific locations, check the symbols that appear on the **legend**. The **compass** shows directions.

Here is a map of Spanish settlement of Arizona and New Mexico.

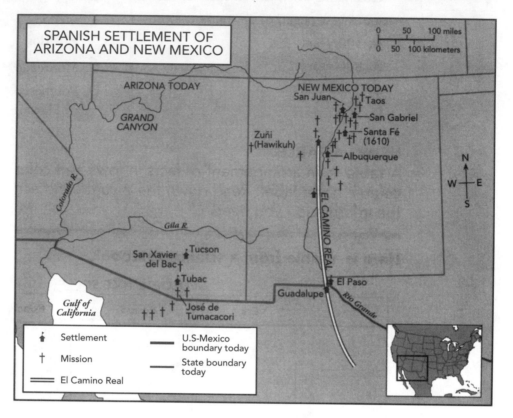

Use the map to answer questions 5–6.

5. Ⓐ Ⓑ Ⓒ Ⓓ
6. Ⓐ Ⓑ Ⓒ Ⓓ

5. How long was the journey along El Camino Real from El Paso to Albuquerque?

   A. about 230 miles

   B. about 150 miles

   C. about 180 miles

   D. about 280 miles

6. Most of the missions in what is now New Mexico

   A. are in the northwestern corner of the state.

   B. are near the Mexican border.

   C. were along El Camino Real.

   D. were near the Rio Grande.

7. Imagine you were traveling by horseback from San Juan to Zuñi by way of Albuquerque. Describe the directions and distances you would travel.

_____

_____

_____

Research and Study Skills

Research and study skills are very important in understanding informational texts. You can use specific parts of your textbooks to help you find the information you need. You can also use other resources to add to your information base.

Tips for Success
- Information on the same topic can appear in different places in a book.
- If the index topic you're looking for isn't there, check for similar or related words or topics.

USING AN ENCYCLOPEDIA INDEX

When researching a topic, the encyclopedia is a good place to get an overview. The **encyclopedia index** lists every reference to a topic in all the volumes of the encyclopedia. The index lists all the articles that mention a certain name or topic. The index uses boldfaced type to list the letter of the volume and the page number where the article can be found.

> **Acid dye**
>   Dye (Synthetic Dyes) **D:320**
> **Acid rain A:24**
>   Environmental Pollution (Other Kinds of Pollution) **E:260**
>   Rain (Variations in Rainfall) **R:144**
>   Water Pollution (Industrial Wastes) **W:108**
> **Acid test** [geology]
>   Mineral (Other Identification Tests) **M:479**

1. To compare the seriousness of acid rain with other types of pollution, such as air pollution, you might first check

   A. Volume A, page 24.

   B. Volume.E, page 260.

   C. Volume R, page 144.

   D. Volume W, page 108.

1. Ⓐ Ⓑ Ⓒ Ⓓ **Mark your answer choice by filling in the oval.**

✓ **Now check to see whether you chose the correct answer.**

   A. Volume A has the main article on acid rain, but it probably isn't the best place to compare kinds of pollution.

   B. This is the correct answer. This would be the best place to look first.

   C. This article focuses on rainfall, not water pollution.

   D. The emphasis here is on water pollution. It would be a good place to check second.

Look back at the encyclopedia index to answer questions 1–2.

1. A B C D
2. A B C D

1. For a general description of the causes and effects of acid rain, you would first check
   A. Volume A, page 24.
   B. Volume E, page 260.
   C. Volume R, page 144.
   D. Volume W, page 108.

2. Which volume might be MOST LIKELY to have information on whether the amount of rainfall affects its acidity?
   A. Volume A
   B. Volume E
   C. Volume R
   D. Volume W

USING A BOOK INDEX

After reading an encyclopedia article, you can use nonfiction books to research a topic in more depth. To find specific information in a book, go to the index first. The **index** is an alphabetical listing of topics covered in a book and all the pages in the book where the topic appears.

Here is the beginning of an index from a book about acid rain.

Acid deposition, 19
Acidity, 20–22
Acid rain
    composition, 19–20
    and crops, 46–47
    formation, 36–37
    and humans, 53–59
    and lakes, 51–53, 62–63,
        67–68, 70–71, 73–74, 78–80

    and laws, 16–19
    and monumental decay, 56–59
    in polar regions, 45–46
    and soil, 47–51
    and tap water, 65–66
    and trees, 40–42, 85–86, 92
Adirondack Mountains, 13–14, 51

Use the book index to answer questions 3–4.

3. A B C D
4. A B C D

3. To find out how acid rain affects our drinking water, you might refer to pages
   A. 16–19.
   B. 45–46.
   C. 65–66.
   D. 78–80.

4. The Acid Precipitation Act of 1980, an early step to counter acid rain, might be mentioned on pages
   A. 16–19.
   B. 53–59.
   C. 13–14.
   D. 78–80.

5. Which topics would you check in the index if you wanted to find out how acid rain affects the world's water supply?

_____

_____

USING THE COMPUTER CATALOG

Most libraries are replacing their card catalogs with **computer catalogs**. By typing in the topic you're researching, you can find out about the books in the library that might provide the information you need.

If you typed in acid rain, you might find these listings.

Author: Firestone, Julia
Title: *The Challenge of Acid Rain*
Publication: Chicago: Environment Publishers, 1998
Description: 285 pp

Call Number	Material	Status
363.78	book	on shelf

Author: Bright, Harvey
Title: *Hard Rain Falling: An Illustrated Guide to the Ravages of Acid Rain*
Publication: New York: Issues, Inc., 1992
Description: 128 pp

Call Number	Material	Status
363.734	book	on shelf

Editors: Windstrom, Lars *et. al.*
Title: *Experimental Research on Acid Precipitation: Selected Readings*
Publication: London: Science Associates, 1991
Description: 456 pp

Call Number	Material	Status
363.731	book	on shelf

Author: Gans, Gertie
Title: *What You Can Do About Acid Rain*
Publication: New York: Take Action Press, 1988
Description: 64 pp

Call Number	Material	Status
363.732	book	out on loan

Use the computer catalog listings to answer questions 6–9.

6. (A) (B) (C) (D)
7. (A) (B) (C) (D)
8. (A) (B) (C) (D)
9. (A) (B) (C) (D)

6. Which book would PROBABLY have the most up-to-date factual information about acid rain?

   A. *The Challenge of Acid Rain*

   B. *Experimental Research on Acid Precipitation: Selected Readings*

   C. *Hard Rain Falling*

   D. *What You Can Do About Acid Rain*

7. Which book would PROBABLY contain the most technical information?

   A. *The Challenge of Acid Rain*

   B. *Experimental Research on Acid Precipitation: Selected Readings*

   C. *Hard Rain Falling*

   D. *What You Can Do About Acid Rain*

8. If you wanted dramatic visuals of the impact of acid rain, you might check

   A. *The Challenge of Acid Rain.*

   B. *Experimental Research on Acid Precipitation: Selected Readings.*

   C. *Hard Rain Falling.*

   D. *What You Can Do About Acid Rain.*

9. Which book is currently unavailable in the library?

   A. *The Challenge of Acid Rain*

   B. *Experimental Research on Acid Precipitation: Selected Readings*

   C. *Hard Rain Falling*

   D. *What You Can Do About Acid Rain*

Chapter Test Informational Text

In these pages, you can use the skills you have practiced in this chapter. Read the passage about acid rain by Laurence Pringle and answer the questions. Mark your answer choices by filling in the ovals.

Rain of Troubles

1. Unpolluted rainwater tends to be slightly acidic. We know this partly as a result of analysis of snow that fell on Greenland more than 180 years ago. Cores of glacial ice reveal that Greenland snow in the early 1800s had little or no acidity. It measured between 6 and 7.6 on the pH scale—the common measure of the relative acidity or alkalinity of matter. The pH scale runs from 0 to 14, with numbers close to 0 highly acidic and those close to 14 the most alkaline. The scale is also logarithmic, so each change of one pH unit represents a chemical change of ten times. In other words, pH 4 is ten times more acidic than pH 5, and pH 3 is one hundred times (ten times ten) more acidic than pH 5 . . . .

2. Beginning in the late nineteenth century, snow deposited in Greenland's glaciers became more acidic as a result of industrialization in the Northern Hemisphere. Coal was the main fuel of many industries, and coal contains sulfur. Coal burning produces sulfur dioxide,

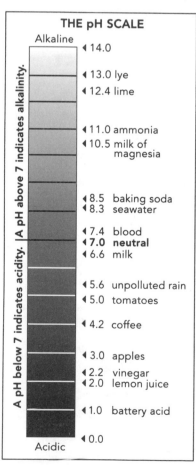

THE pH SCALE

Alkaline
- 14.0
- 13.0 lye
- 12.4 lime
- 11.0 ammonia
- 10.5 milk of magnesia
- 8.5 baking soda
- 8.3 seawater
- 7.4 blood
- **7.0 neutral**
- 6.6 milk
- 5.6 unpolluted rain
- 5.0 tomatoes
- 4.2 coffee
- 3.0 apples
- 2.2 vinegar
- 2.0 lemon juice
- 1.0 battery acid
- 0.0

Acidic

A pH above 7 indicates alkalinity. | A pH below 7 indicates acidity.

which in the atmosphere may be converted to sulfuric acid.

3. In 1872, British chemist Robert Angus Smith studied the heavily polluted air of London and coined the term *acid rain.* In his book *Air and Rain: The Beginnings of a Chemical Climatology,* Smith wrote, "Acidity is caused almost entirely by sulphuric acid, which may come from coal or the oxidation of sulphur compounds from decomposition . . . . The presence of free sulphuric acid in the air sufficiently explains the fading of colours in prints and dyed goods, the rusting of metals, and the rotting of blinds." Smith also noted that acid rain eroded the stone of buildings, particularly in the lower parts where rainwater accumulated. His observations were sound but were largely ignored.

4. Eighty years passed before another scientist, Eville Gorham, investigated the phenomenon of acid rain. Gorham stumbled upon it by accident, while studying the ecology of peat bogs in the 1950s. In order to understand the nutrition of bog plants in England's Lake District, he began to collect and analyze rainwater. "The minute I started analysing the rain," he recalled, "I found that we were alternately dosed with sea salt when the winds blew from the Irish Sea and with acid from the winds that blew up from industrial Lancaster."

5. Like Robert Angus Smith's book, the research of Eville Gorham caused no concern when he published his findings in 1955. This was before the 1962 publication of Rachel Carson's *Silent Spring*, before the birth of the environmental movement, before the public became conscious of the harmful side effects of technological developments. Scientists were, however, starting to study the chemical composition of the atmosphere.

6. Even before Gorham began his work, agricultural scientists had set up a rain-sampling network in Europe. Their goal was to discover what chemicals were in precipitation, in order to discover whether airborne chemicals actually fertilized crops. Precipitation was collected at more than a hundred stations in northern and western Europe, and the data gave a record of changes in pH over that region.

7. In 1961 a Swedish scientist named Svante Odén began to collect water samples from lakes and rivers. After a few years he saw a clear connection between changes in the chemistry of these surface waters and those in the chemistry of rain collected in the European sampling network. The rainfall over northern Europe had become more acidic. And as the acidity of precipitation increased, so did the acidity of Scandinavian lakes and rivers. This increase coincided with increased burning of coal and other fossil fuels in central Europe and Great Britain.

8. In the spring of 1967 Odén received a call from a fisheries inspector who told of Swedish lakes in which fish were dying and others in which they had disappeared. The pH measurements of the lakes seemed much lower than normal. Could there be a connection? . . .

9. The decline of fish and other aquatic life in Sweden and Norway had actually been under way for decades. Unexplained kills of Atlantic salmon had been reported as early as 1911. Brown trout began disappearing from mountain lakes in the 1920s and 1930s. By the 1950s many lakes in southern Norway were lifeless, but no one could explain these losses. Svante Odén was the first person to link this damage to pollutants carried long distances by air. He also raised questions about other possible effects of acid rain—on soils, forest trees, and other plants. When his findings were published in 1968, the menace of acid rain, (first described by Smith in 1872) finally caught public and scientific attention.

10. The Swedish government began its own study of acid precipitation and it presented the results at the 1972 United Nations Conference on the Human Environment, held in Stockholm. This international conference was an apt forum at which to present the Swedish report entitled "Air Pollution across National Boundaries." Seventy-seven percent of the acid precipitation falling on southern Sweden came from other countries—a "form of **unpremeditated** chemical warfare."

11. Sweden's report also warned that acid precipitation might be affecting parts of Canada and the northeastern United States. Neither nation, however, had a network of stations where precipitation was collected and analyzed. Few data were available to show how the acidity of rain might have changed over decades in North America.

12. Among the earliest measurements of precipitation pH in the United States were those made in 1939, in the state of Maine. The pH was 5.9—the slightly acidic condition of unpolluted rain.

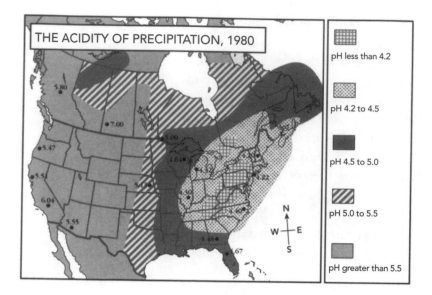

THE ACIDITY OF PRECIPITATION, 1980

pH less than 4.2

pH 4.2 to 4.5

pH 4.5 to 5.0

pH 5.0 to 5.5

pH greater than 5.5

Between 1959 and 1966, agencies of the United States government took monthly precipitation samples across the nation. Chemists commonly found pH values above 6.5 west of the Mississippi, with much more acidic readings in the East. Not until the mid-1970s, however, did the United States and Canada set up a long-term program for studying the chemistry of precipitation.

1. Ⓐ Ⓑ Ⓒ Ⓓ
2. Ⓐ Ⓑ Ⓒ Ⓓ
3. Ⓐ Ⓑ Ⓒ Ⓓ
4. Ⓐ Ⓑ Ⓒ Ⓓ

CENTRAL PURPOSE

1. The author's central purpose for writing this passage is

    A. to identify the main causes of acid rain.

    B. to point out the serious environmental damage done by acid rain.

    C. to outline the process by which scientists became aware of acid rain.

    D. to identify areas of the world where acid rain is a problem.

MAJOR IDEA

2. What is the major idea of paragraph 3?

    A. While studying London's air pollution, Robert Angus Smith coined the term acid rain.

    B. Acid rain is caused almost entirely by sulfuric acid.

    C. The causes and effects of acid rain were known but ignored for 100 years.

    D. Acid rain has damaged prints, dyed goods, stone buildings, and other objects.

MAJOR IDEA

3. What is the major idea of paragraphs 10 and 11?

    A. Most of Sweden's acid rain came from sources outside its boundaries.

    B. The United Nations is an ideal forum for dealing with the problems of acid rain.

    C. Sweden led the way in researching and publicizing the issue of acid rain.

    D. The United States and Canada collected less data on acidity levels than Europe.

SUPPORTING DETAILS

4. The scientist who played the most significant role in alerting the world to the problem of acid rain was

    A. Robert Angus Smith.

    B. Eville Gorham.

    C. Rachel Carson.

    D. Svante Odén.

SUPPORTING DETAILS

5. Which detail BEST supports the major idea of paragraph 12?

   A. The pH level of precipitation in Maine was 5.9.

   B. Beginning in 1959, the U.S. government took monthly precipitation samples.

   C. More acidic readings were found in the eastern United States.

   D. Maine was the first state to measure precipitation pH.

TABLE

6. According to the pH scale on p. 38, apples are *less* acidic than

   A. unpolluted rain.

   B. coffee.

   C. lemon juice.

   D. milk.

MAP

7. According to the map on p. 40, which region has precipitation with a pH 5.0 to 5.5?

   A. Eastern United States

   B. the West coast

   C. Central United States

   D. Northwestern United States

VOCABULARY

8. The word **unpremeditated** in paragraph 10 means

   A. unplanned.

   B. unforgivable.

   C. ineffective.

   D. nonviolent.

BOOK INDEX

9. Which pages listed in the part of the index shown below might tell about U.S. laws and regulations that limit acid rain?

   > *Environment*, 13–14
   > environmentalists, 90, 91, 95, 103–105
   > Environmental Protection Agency (EPA),
   >   22–26, 69–75, 84–86
   > eutrophication, 53–54
   > Experimental Lakes Area (Canada)
   >   40–42

   A. 13–14

   B. 90, 91, 95, 103–105

   C. 22–26, 69–75, 84–86

   D. 53–54

ENCYCLOPEDIA INDEX

10. Which volume of the encyclopedia would MOST LIKELY tell about "scrubbers," machines that remove pollutants from coal smoke before it enters the atmosphere?

    > Acid rain A:24
    >   Environmental Pollution (Other Kinds
    >   of Pollution) E:260
    >   Fish (Effects on freshwater fish) F: 239
    >   Anti-pollution technology in coal-
    >   burning plants P:324
    >   Water Pollution (Industrial Wastes)
    >   W:108

    A. Volume A, page 24

    B. Volume E, page 260

    C. Volume P, page 324

    D. Volume R, page 144

5. Ⓐ Ⓑ Ⓒ Ⓓ
6. Ⓐ Ⓑ Ⓒ Ⓓ
7. Ⓐ Ⓑ Ⓒ Ⓓ
8. Ⓐ Ⓑ Ⓒ Ⓓ
9. Ⓐ Ⓑ Ⓒ Ⓓ
10. Ⓐ Ⓑ Ⓒ Ⓓ

11. Why is "creeping catastrophe" a good description of the acid rain problem?

_____

_____

_____

 STOP

Persuasive text will also appear on most reading tests. Here are some common questions about persuasive reading passages.

 What is a persuasive text?
A persuasive text is a piece of writing that attempts to convince you to act or think in a certain way.

 What types of reading materials are persuasive texts?
Speeches are a common type of persuasive text, and newspaper editorials and letters to the editor are usually persuasive too. Advertisements in newspapers and magazines are another type of persuasive text.

 What are the major elements of a persuasive text?
A persuasive text contains a main idea and supporting details. Usually a persuasive text uses facts and opinions to make its main point. In addition, persuasive texts may use comparison in an effort to influence the reader. Finally, many authors use specific persuasive techniques that appeal to the reader's emotions.

- The **main idea** is the most important idea in a passage of text.
- The **supporting details** in a persuasive text develop the main ideas.
- A **fact** is a statement known to be true or something that can be checked or proven. An **opinion** is a statement that expresses a personal judgment, feeling, or belief.
- **Comparison** shows the ways in which things are similar or alike. **Contrast** shows the ways things differ.
- Some common **persuasive techniques** are loaded language, name-calling, exaggeration, and bandwagon appeal.

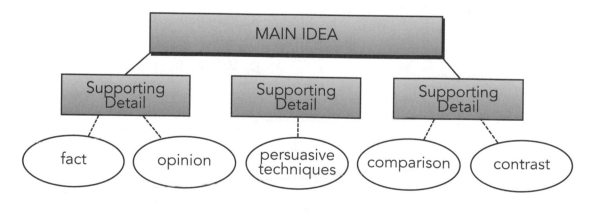

Test Questions About Persuasive Text

Many test questions about persuasive text focus on the main idea that the author presents. You will also be asked to identify the supporting details that develop or tell about the main ideas. Other questions ask you to distinguish between facts and opinions. The questions below, which are taken from actual tests, will help you become familiar with the most common types of questions about persuasive texts.

Questions About the Main Idea

- Which statement BEST expresses the main idea of this editorial?
- What does the writer of this letter urge all citizens to do?
- With which statement would the author PROBABLY agree?

Questions About Supporting Details

- Which of these details supports the main idea of the editorial?
- Which of these additional facts support the author's main point?
- Which detail about the mayor's last term would the speech writer probably NOT include?

Questions About Fact and Opinion

- Which of the following statements is a fact?
- Which of the following statements could be proven true?
- Which of the following statements is an opinion?

Questions About Comparison and Contrast

- Unlike most garden apartment complexes, Greenville Estates offers all residents which of the following _____.
- Why does the writer contrast the activities of a typical mother today with her counterpart of 100 years ago?

Questions About Persuasive Techniques

- Which phrase in paragraph 3 is an example of name-calling?
- The author exaggerates the truth when she says: _____.
- Which is an example of the persuasive technique called bandwagon appeal?
- Which paragraph contains loaded language?

The lessons in Chapter 3 will help you understand how to answer test questions about persuasive text. You'll read short passages of persuasive text that illustrate main ideas and supporting details as well as facts and opinions. You'll also have a chance to work with passages that use comparison and contrast and other persuasive techniques.

Main Idea and Supporting Details

A persuasive text often takes the form of speeches, editorials, and letters. Excerpts of persuasive writing on tests usually contain one main idea. The **main idea** is the most important idea in a paragraph or passage. This is the main point that the author wants you to accept.

Supporting details develop or tell more about the main idea of a passage. In persuasive text, writers include supporting details that will make their main ideas more appealing or convincing. The details in a persuasive text help convince readers that the main idea is "right."

Tips for Success
- Figure out the main idea and decide which details support it.
- Decide which details are the most persuasive.

Rosa Parks was a leader of the Civil Rights Movement. In this letter to a student, she shares her feelings about the importance of hope.

Elizabeth, many times we as adults seek to teach students like you without giving you examples of what the true meanings of words are so that you can learn from them.

Hope is wanting something that means a lot to you. It is like wanting something that you do not have. Hope is something we feel with our hearts. When we hope for something with out hearts, it becomes an expectation.

Hope is also something we believe in. Many people I have known believed in ending racial segregation in this country, and their hope that it could happen influenced their actions and brought about change. A friend of mine, the Reverend Jesse Jackson, says, "We must keep hope alive." I agree. You can help keep hope alive by believing in yourself. Your hope for yourself and for the future can make this world a better place to live.

—Dear Mrs. Parks: A Dialogue with Today's Youth

1. What is Rosa Parks's main idea about hope?

    A. Many students aren't given good examples of hope.

    B. We must keep hope alive or our future will be dark indeed.

    C. Having hopes that we believe in will make the world a better place.

    D. The struggle to end segregation was possible because people hoped and believed it was possible.

1. Ⓐ Ⓑ Ⓒ Ⓓ   **Mark your answer choice by filling in the oval.**

✔ **Now check to see whether you chose the correct answer.**

    A. Rosa Parks opens with this comment, but it isn't her main idea.

    B. Rosa Parks doesn't really talk about a dark future without hope.

    C. This is the correct answer. It best expresses the main idea of the letter.

    D. Rosa Parks uses this struggle as an example to support her main idea.

This is an excerpt from an editorial written by Eleanor Roosevelt on the day before Election Day in 1950. Roosevelt played an important role in establishing the United Nations. As you read, think about the main point she makes.

November 2—I think we need to change completely our type of campaigning . . . . a sum of money could be given every candidate to cover the needed educational services which should be the basis of any campaign in a democracy.

It is important for the people to be educated as to their candidates' qualifications and as to the issues and beliefs of the various parties.

In a democracy it should be part of the obligation of every voter to obtain this amount of knowledge before an election . . . . The next obligation is to make sure that we vote. If we don't vote, then we cannot complain when the power of the government gets into the hands of a few, sometimes corrupt, individuals.

The average citizen of a democracy does not fulfill his obligations on Election Day. He must try to follow the record of those for whom he voted. He must write them now and then and make them feel that he is an interested citizen . . . .

This is our business, whether it is what happens in our local community, or in our state, or in our nation, and now even if it is what our delegates stand for in the United Nations.

— *Eleanor Roosevelt's My Day, Volume II: The Post-War Years*

---

1. Ⓐ Ⓑ Ⓒ Ⓓ
2. Ⓐ Ⓑ Ⓒ Ⓓ

Mark the best answer for questions 1–2.

1. What is the main idea of this passage from Eleanor Roosevelt's editorial?

   A. Citizens must know more about what their delegates to the United Nations stand for.

   B. The United States should give money to political candidates.

   C. Educating voters should be the basis of a political campaign.

   D. American citizens must be well-informed and active in government.

2. With which statement would Eleanor Roosevelt be MOST LIKELY to agree?

   A. Democracy is not a spectator sport.

   B. Individuals can have little impact in these days of big government.

   C. Government should play no role in political campaigns.

   D. The American campaign system is the best in the world.

3. In your opinion, what ways is the business of government "our business"?

_____

_____

_____

Fact and Opinion

Writers of persuasive texts use facts and opinions to argue their points. On tests, you will have to distinguish between these two types of statements. Distinguishing between facts and opinions will also help you judge the strength of a persuasive argument.

A **fact** is a statement known to be true or something that can be checked or proven. You can check the factual information in reference books or other sources. An **opinion** is a statement that expresses a personal judgment, feeling, or belief. Opinions cannot be checked and proven to be true. Opinions often contain words such as *believe*, *best*, *better*, *worse*, *should*, and *probably*.

Tips for Success

- To spot facts, ask yourself if a statement could be checked or proven.
- To spot opinions, look for words that show values, like *worst* or *best*.
- Ask yourself, "Why does the author include this fact? Why this opinion?"

As you read this passage, look for facts and opinions.

One of the earliest mass-produced television sets in America, made by the Pilot Radio Corporation, looked like a bank safe. The screen sat behind heavy doors that could be locked shut. The idea was that if this new machine proved *too* alluring, if it seemed to hold the family under its spell, parents could bolt up the set and hide the key. The set didn't sell.

Some people would still like to put a lock on television. Their reasons are familiar. Television is violent. It's boring. It traffics in dumb situations and easy laughs. It stereotypes everyone. It turns viewers into "vidiots" with short attention spans. It's cluttered with ads that urge people to buy things they don't need . . . .

—Marian Calabro, *Zap!: A Brief History of Television*

1. Which statement BEST describes the author's use of facts and opinions?
   A. The first paragraph is mainly facts while the second is largely opinions.
   B. Neither paragraph contains any facts.
   C. The first paragraph is mainly opinions while the second is mainly facts.
   D. Both paragraphs contain about an equal number of facts and opinions.

1. Ⓐ Ⓑ Ⓒ Ⓓ

Mark your answer choice by filling in the oval.

Now check to see whether you chose the correct answer.

   A. This is the correct answer. Three of the four sentences in the first paragraph are facts while most of the second paragraph is opinion.
   B. The account of the early "safe" television is a fact. You could check to see when and where it was built.
   C. The statements in the second paragraph, such as "It's boring" and "It stereotypes everyone" are opinions. There's no way to prove them.
   D. The first paragraph uses both facts and opinions. The second paragraph is primarily opinion.

As you read this passage from a book by former President Jimmy Carter, look for facts and opinions.

As much as we may not like to admit it, there are many malnourished people in our country, despite the enormous surplus of food produced on American farms and ranches. Another, often related social problem has grown so serious that few Americans can ignore it: homelessness.

In the richest American cities, people without homes can be seen living on the streets and standing in line for food at soup kitchens or for beds in temporary shelters. It is estimated that there are sixty thousand homeless people in New York City, twelve thousand in Atlanta, and like numbers in other metropolitan areas. Thousands of other people live in substandard private shelters and government housing developments. The numbers increase each year, with more and more women and children among those without decent dwellings. An average of one hundred thousand children in America sleep on the streets or in temporary shelters every night.

One of the main problems that homeless people face is stigma, which literally means a mark or brand of shame. Some more privileged members of society label the homeless on sight as unworthy, lazy, or even worse—as drug users and thieves. While it is true that some homeless people are lazy, and others are addicted to drugs and alcohol, many have only lost their jobs and are unable to afford a place to live. Some of them are parents with small children. And still others are mentally ill, which carries an additional stigma. New York City estimates that fully one-third of its homeless people are severely mentally ill. Our wealthy society should realize that a decent place to live is a basic human right for all its citizens, especially for those who are unable to care for themselves.

—*Talking Peace: A Vision for the Next Generation*

1. ⒶⒷⒸⒹ
2. ⒶⒷⒸⒹ

Mark the best answer for questions 1–2.

1. Which statement is an opinion?

   A. Another problem has grown so serious that few Americans can ignore it: homelessness.

   B. It is estimated that there are twelve thousand homeless people in Atlanta.

   C. New York City estimates that fully one-third of its homeless people are severely mentally ill.

   D. More and more women and children are among those without decent dwellings.

2. Which statement is a fact?

   A. Our wealthy society should realize that a decent place to live is a basic human right.

   B. One of the main problems that homeless people face is stigma.

   C. Thousands of people live in substandard private shelters.

   D. It is true that some homeless people are lazy.

Lesson 3 Comparison and Contrast

Persuasive texts that are organized by **comparison** and **contrast** are often one-sided. For example, a letter writer in favor of school uniforms would probably mention all the advantages that uniforms provide and all the problems that arise when students wear whatever they like. It's unlikely, however, that the letter would go into problems caused by uniforms or the advantages of allowing students to choose their clothing.

Tips for Success

- Decide what is being compared in a persuasive text.
- Determine which points of comparison support the writer's main idea.

As you read this passage, note how the author Gilbert M. Grosvenor contrasts 1988 with 1888, the year his magazine, _National Geographic_, was founded.

We live in a changed world from that of 1888, and we are a changed nation. Our founders knew an America with rising expectations, while we see a superpower riddled with self-doubt. Tropical rain forests were a mysterious challenge in 1888. The challenge in 1988 is saving them from disappearance. Automobiles had just been invented, and airplanes were unknown. Would our founders be impressed by rush-hour traffic, a brown cloud over Denver, or aerial gridlock at Chicago's O'Hare Airport? Could they have conceived of a Mexico City with 20 million people in an atmosphere so murky that the sun is obscured, so poisonous that school is sometimes delayed until late morning, when the air clears?

—"Will We Mend Our Earth?"

1. What is the main persuasive point that the author makes by contrasting 1988 with 1888?

   A. The developments of the last 100 years have brought both advantages and disadvantages.

   B. The people of 1888 would be amazed at the changes that have taken place over the last 100 years.

   C. A century of technological development has created an environmental crisis.

   D. The world was a better place 100 years ago.

1. Ⓐ Ⓑ Ⓒ Ⓓ **Mark your answer choice by filling in the oval.**

✔ **Now check to see whether you chose the correct answer.**

   A. The writer doesn't focus on the advantages that have come with a century of development.

   B. This may be true, but the author does not try to persuade us of this.

   C. This is the correct answer. The author contrasts 1988 unfavorably with 1888 as a way to persuade the reader that we face very serious environmental problems.

   D. The author may imply this, but it is not his main persuasive point.

Test Practice

This speech was given more than 100 years ago by a lawyer whose client was suing a neighbor for having killed his dog. As you read, pay attention to the comparisons he makes.

The best friend a man has in the world may turn against him and become his enemy. His son or daughter that he has reared with loving care may prove ungrateful. Those who are nearest and dearest to us, those whom we trust with our happiness and our good name may become traitors to their faith. The money that a man has, he may lose. It flies away from him, perhaps when he needs it most. A man's reputation may be sacrificed in a moment of ill-considered action. The people who are prone to fall on their knees to do us honor when success is with us may be the first to throw the stone of **malice** when failure settles its cloud upon our heads.

The only absolutely unselfish friend that man can have in this selfish world, the one that never deserts him . . . is his dog. A man's dog stands by him in prosperity and in poverty, in health and in sickness. He will sleep on the cold ground, where the wintry winds blow and the snow drives fiercely, if only he may be near his master's side. . . . He guards the sleep of his pauper master as if he were a prince. When all other friends desert, he remains. When riches take wings, and reputation falls to pieces, he is as constant in his love as the sun in its journey through the heavens.

—George Graham Vest, *Lend Me Your Ears: Great Speeches in History*

---

1. Ⓐ Ⓑ Ⓒ Ⓓ
2. Ⓐ Ⓑ Ⓒ Ⓓ
3. Ⓐ Ⓑ Ⓒ Ⓓ

Mark the best answer for questions 1–3.

1. The examples given in the first paragraph are PROBABLY meant to persuade the audience that:
   A. A dog's devotion cannot be taken for granted.
   B. Friends, children, and dogs are more faithful than fame and fortune.
   C. Life isn't worth living without the companionship of a dog.
   D. Nothing in life is as dependable as a dog.

2. In the second paragraph, the author compares a dog to
   A. a prince.
   B. great riches.
   C. the sun.
   D. the journey of life.

3. The word **malice** means
   A. hatred.
   B. concern.
   C. value.
   D. disregard.

4. How might this speech have affected the jury that was trying the case?

_____

_____

_____

Persuasive Techniques

To make their texts persuasive, authors use a variety of techniques.

- **Loaded language** takes advantage of the strong positive or negative feelings or emotions that people associate with certain words.
  The proposed law will destroy our freedom of speech.

- **Name-calling** labels someone or something in a negative way.
  My opponent is a crackpot and a liar.

- **Exaggeration** is enlarging something beyond the truth.
  You won't find a better deal in the universe!

- **Bandwagon appeal** tries to persuade you to do something by emphasizing that a great many others are doing so.
  Isn't it time you joined everyone at Paradise Health Club?

Tips for Success

- Look for the persuasive techniques that an author uses.
- Remember that loaded language makes use of positive or negative word associations.
- Watch out for exaggeration and the "everybody's doing it" argument.

Look for persuasive techniques in this passage from a speech that Senator Everett Dirksen presented to Congress in an unsuccessful effort to make the marigold the national flower.

The marigold is a native of North America and can in truth and in fact be called an American flower.

It is national in character, for it grows and thrives in every one of the fifty states of this nation. It conquers the extremes of temperature. It well withstands the summer sun and the evening chill.

Its robustness reflects the hardihood and character of the generations who pioneered and built this land into a great nation. It is not temperamental about fertility. It resists its natural enemies, the insects. It is self-reliant and requires little attention. Its spectacular colors—lemon and orange, rich brown and deep mahogany—befit the imaginative qualities of this nation.

1. "Self-reliant" and "generations who pioneered and built this land" are BEST described as examples of which persuasive technique?

   A. loaded language

   B. name-calling

   C. exaggeration

   D. bandwagon appeal

1. Ⓐ Ⓑ Ⓒ Ⓓ **Mark your answer choice by filling in the oval.**

✓ **Now check to see whether you chose the correct answer.**

   A. This is the correct answer. The words have positive connotations.

   B. Name-calling is negative, and the author is positive about marigolds.

   C. The author may exaggerate the qualities of marigolds somewhat, but he is mainly using loaded language with positive connotations.

   D. The author doesn't suggest that "everybody" is doing something.

Test Practice

Read this excerpt from a May 1941 speech by Secretary of the Interior Harold Ickes. The speaker wanted to persuade his listeners that the United States should go to war against the Nazis in Europe.

No, liberty never dies. The Genghis Khans come and go. The Attilas come and go. The Hitlers flash and sputter out. But freedom endures.

Destroy a whole generation of those who have known how to walk erect in . . . free air, and the next generation will rise against the oppressors and restore freedom. Today in Europe, the Nazi Attila may gloat that he has destroyed democracy. He is wrong. In small farmhouses all over Central Europe, in the shops of Germany and Italy, on the docks of Holland and Belgium, freedom still lives in the hearts of men. It will endure like a hardy tree gone into the wintertime, awaiting the spring.

And, like spring, spreading from the South into Scandinavia, the democratic revolution will come . . . . These men and women, hundreds of millions of them, now in bondage or threatened with slavery, are our comrades and our allies. They are only waiting for our leadership and our encouragement, for the spark that we can supply.

These hundreds of millions of liberty-loving people, now oppressed . . . have the will to destroy the Nazi gangsters . . . .

We will help brave England drive back the hordes . . . who besiege her, and then we will join for the destruction of savage and bloodthirsty dictators everywhere. But we must be firm and decisive. We must know our will and make it felt. And we must hurry.

Mark the best answer for questions 1–4.

1. A B C D
2. A B C D
3. A B C D
4. A B C D

1. Which phrase from the second paragraph is NOT an example of loaded language?
   A. "the Nazi Attila may gloat"
   B. "he is wrong"
   C. "rise against the oppressors"
   D. "freedom still lives"

2. The speech uses the bandwagon appeal when it describes the
   A. "savage and bloodthirsty" dictators.
   B. need to hurry to help England.
   C. the hundreds of millions of Europeans who are our allies.
   D. the whole generation that has had its freedom destroyed.

3. Describing the Nazis as "gangsters" is
   A. loaded language.
   B. name-calling.
   C. bandwagon appeal.
   D. exaggeration.

4. Why did the author use the exaggeration "savage and bloodthirsty" to describe dictators?
   A. He wanted to make the Nazis sound worse than they were.
   B. He was running for office and wanted to sound patriotic.
   C. He didn't like Hitler.
   D. He needed to convince the United States of the seriousness of the situation.

Read the two essays. Then use the skills you have practiced in Chapter 3 to answer the questions. Mark your answer choices by filling in the ovals.

"The Liberry"
by Bel Kaufman

An immigrant from Russia, Bel Kaufman became an English teacher in New York City and later the author of a best-selling novel about high school life, Up the Down Staircase.

1. A small boy in one of William Saroyan's stories finds himself in the public library for the first time. He looks around in awe: "All them books," he says, "and something written in each one!"

2. I remember myself as a 12-year-old, newly arrived from Russia, groping toward the mastery of the English language in my neighborhood library. Guided by no reading lists, informed by no book reviews, I had no use for the card catalogue, since I worked each shelf alphabetically, burrowing my way from one end of the stacks to the other, relentless as a mole. I read by trial and error, through trash and treasure; like a true addict, I was interested not so much in quality as in getting the stuff.

3. Sometimes I would stumble upon a book that was special; a book unrequired, unrecommended, unspoiled by teacher-imposed chores—"Name 3 . . . . Answer the following . . . "—a book to be read for sheer pleasure.

4. Where else was it allowed, even encouraged, to thumb through a book, to linger on a page without being shooed away from handling the merchandise? This was merchandise to be handled. I was not fooled by the stiff, impassive maroon and dark-green library bindings; I nosed out the good ones. If the pages were worn and dog-eared, if the card tucked into its paper pocket inside the cover was stamped with lots of dates, I knew I had a winner.

5. Those dates linked me to the anonymous fellowship of other readers whose hands had turned the pages I was turning, who sometimes left penciled clues in the margins: a philosophic "How True!"—a **succinct** "Stinks."

6. Here, within walls built book by solid book, we sat in silent kinship, the only sounds shuffling of feet, scraping of chairs, an occasional loud whisper, and the librarian's stern "Shhh!"

7. The librarian was always there, unobtrusive and omniscient, ready for any question: Where to find a book about Eskimos? A history of submarines? A best-selling novel?—unruffled even by a request I once overheard in the children's section: "Have you got a book for an eight-year-old with tonsils?"

8. I am remembering this because today the public libraries are becoming less and less available to the people who need them most. Already shut part of the time, their hours reduced by 50 percent in the last five years, their budgets further curtailed as of July 1, and still threatened with continued cuts in staff and services, the public libraries have suffered more in the city's financial squeeze than any other major public-service agencies.

9. The first priority of our nation, according to former New York State Commissioner of Education, James E. Allen, is the right to read. Educators are inundating our schools with massive surveys, innovative techniques and expensive gimmicks to combat illiteracy and improve the reading skills of our children—at the same time that our public libraries are gradually closing their doors.

10. What are our priorities? Name 3.

11. It seems to me that especially now, when there are so many people in our city whose language is not English, whose homes are barren of books, who are daily seduced by clamorous offers of instant diversion, especially now we must hold on to something that will endure when the movie is over, the television set broken, the class dismissed for the last time.

12. For many, the public library is the only quiet place in an unquiet world; a refuge from the violence and ugliness outside; the only space available for privacy of work or thought. For many it is the only exposure to books waiting on open shelves to be taken home, free of charge.

13. As a former student put it: "In a liberry, it's hard to avoid reading."

14. When I taught English in high school, I used to ask my students to bring a library card to class, on the chance that if they had one they might use it. One boy brought in his aunt's. "Aw, I ain't gonna use it," he cheerfully assured me, "I just brought it to *show* you!"

15. Still—some did make use of their cards, if only because they were *there*. Some enter the library today because it is *there*. Inside are all them books, and something written in each one. How sad for our city if the sign on the door should say CLOSED.

What the Library Means to Me
by Amy Tan

Amy Tan, the best-selling author of such novels as The Joy Luck Club, *wrote this essay when she was 8 years old.*

1. My name is Amy Tan, 8 years old, a third grader in Matanzas School. It is brand new school and everything is so nice and pretty. I love school because the many things I learn seem to turn on a light in the little room in my mind. I can see a lot of things I have never seen before. I can read many interesting books by myself now. I love to read. My father takes me to the library every two weeks, and I check five or six books each time. These books seem to open many windows in my little room. I can see many wonderful things outside. I always look forward to go the library.

2. Once my father did not take me to the library for a whole month. He said, the library was closed because the building is too old. I missed it like a good friend. It seems a long long time my father took me to the library again just before Christmas. Now it is on the second floor of some stores. I wish we can have a real nice and pretty library like my school. I put 18 cents in the box and signed my name to join Citizens of Santa Rosa Library.

1. Ⓐ Ⓑ Ⓒ Ⓓ
2. Ⓐ Ⓑ Ⓒ Ⓓ
3. Ⓐ Ⓑ Ⓒ Ⓓ
4. Ⓐ Ⓑ Ⓒ Ⓓ
5. Ⓐ Ⓑ Ⓒ Ⓓ
6. Ⓐ Ⓑ Ⓒ Ⓓ

MAIN IDEA

1. What is the main idea of Ms. Kaufman's essay?

   A. Teenagers and newcomers to America should get into the habit of reading more.

   B. Libraries are good places to continue our education.

   C. We must make sure that libraries are open and available to all.

   D. Libraries and librarians do not receive the appreciation they deserve.

SUPPORTING DETAILS

2. In making her main point, the author shares her childhood memories

   A. to provide an entertaining picture of immigrant life.

   B. to show how libraries can play a powerful role in people's lives.

   C. to explain how young people should regard books.

   D. to urge libraries to update their books and provide better services.

MAIN IDEA

3. Readers first become aware of Ms. Kaufman's main purpose for writing in

   A. paragraph 2.

   B. paragraph 7.

   C. paragraph 8.

   D. paragraph 11.

FACT AND OPINION

4. Which statement is a fact?

   A. The librarian was always there, unobtrusive and omniscient.

   B. The city's libraries have had their hours reduced 50 percent in the last five years.

   C. If the pages were worn-out and dog-eared, I knew I had a winner.

   D. The first priority of our nation is the right to read.

COMPARISON/CONTRAST

5. In paragraphs 11 and 12 of Ms. Kaufman's essay, the author contrasts the library with the world outside in order to emphasize

   A. that the library is only one of many places where on-going education occurs.

   B. that homeless people often find shelter in libraries.

   C. that people must be willing to search for what they want.

   D. that the library is a place of peace and quiet.

FACT AND OPINION

6. Which statement in the essay is an opinion?

   A. A small boy in one of William Saroyan's stories finds himself in the public library for the first time.

   B. Libraries are threatened with further cuts in staff and services.

   C. How sad for our city if the sign on the library door should say CLOSED.

   D. The public library has suffered more budget cuts than any other major public-service agency.

COMPARISON/CONTRAST

7. Like the small boy in William Saroyan's story, Ms. Kaufman at 12 years old was

   A. a newcomer to this country.

   B. trying to escape the ugliness of the world around her.

   C. in awe of the library and its books.

   D. determined to become a writer some day.

PERSUASIVE TECHNIQUES

8. In paragraph 9, Ms. Kaufman writes of "expensive gimmicks" used in school to improve students' reading skills. This phrase is BEST described as

   A. exaggeration.

   B. loaded language.

   C. bandwagon appeal.

   D. name-calling.

VOCABULARY

9. What is the meaning of **succinct** in paragraph 5?

   A. brief

   B. confusing

   C. memorable

   D. foolish

MAIN IDEA

10. Why do you think the author chose the title "The Liberry" instead of "The Library"?

    A. She feels the main purpose of a library is to help people spell correctly.

    B. "Liberry" is a childlike and humorous mispronunciation.

    C. The title emphasizes that the library opens up knowledge to the young and the uneducated.

    D. Without libraries, people will forget what they know and begin to misuse words.

COMPARISON/CONTRAST

11. In paragraph 11, the author uses comparison and contrast to express the idea that

    A. TV and movies play an important role in education.

    B. libraries must include more books written in languages other than English.

    C. in today's culture, many people will find enduring values only in library books.

    D. people must begin to buy books for their homes instead of watching so much TV.

7.	Ⓐ	Ⓑ	Ⓒ	Ⓓ
8.	Ⓐ	Ⓑ	Ⓒ	Ⓓ
9.	Ⓐ	Ⓑ	Ⓒ	Ⓓ
10.	Ⓐ	Ⓑ	Ⓒ	Ⓓ
11.	Ⓐ	Ⓑ	Ⓒ	Ⓓ

12. In what ways does Ms. Tan's essay, written when she was only 8 years old, support the main idea of Ms. Kaufman's essay?

_____

_____

_____

_____

The final type of text that will appear on the reading test is **everyday text**. Here are some questions you might have about this type of text.

 What is everyday text?
Everyday text is reading material that you might use at home, in school, or in the community. Usually it contains information that you need to know in order to accomplish something practical.

 What types of reading materials are everyday texts?
Everyday texts are a common part of your life. Movie schedules, recipes, rules and regulations, directions for making something, food labels, travel brochures, computer manuals—there are literally hundreds of different types of everyday text.

 What are the major elements of an everyday text?
Because everyday texts are so varied, they have different elements.

- The **relevant data** in an everyday text are the details you need to achieve a specific purpose.

- A **sequence of data** is a set of steps that show you the order you need to follow to complete a task.

- Often, you need to organize or **classify** information in everyday text in order to make a choice or reach a logical conclusion.

- Sometimes, you will need to **synthesize** or combine the information from one or more everyday texts to make decisions or judgments.

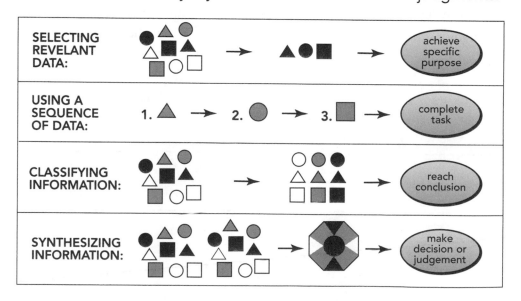

Test Questions About Everyday Text

Many test questions ask you to select relevant details from an everyday text. The test may also ask questions about the sequence in which you would perform certain steps to create something or accomplish a task. Questions about everyday text also ask you to organize and synthesize information in order to make a decision or draw a conclusion. The questions below come from actual tests and show the most common types of questions asked about everyday text.

Questions About Relevant Data

- How many calories are contained in an 8-ounce serving of yogurt?
- When is Flight 4311 scheduled to land at O'Hare Airport?
- How much is a weekday matinee ticket for a seat in Level C?
- Which is NOT an example of strenuous exercise?

Questions About Using a Sequence of Data

- Which step comes first?
- What is the last step in making the rubbing?
- Before beginning mouth-to-mouth resuscitation, the first aid worker should _____.
- When should a bank customer enter his or her personal identification number?

Questions About Classifying Information

- Which travel package seems to be the BEST bargain?
- Why is it important to lift the mixture off the screen slowly?
- If Cameron gets out of class at 11:30 A.M. and must be home by 2:30 P.M., which train must he take?
- What can you learn about the motor bike from information in the ad?

Questions About Synthesizing Information

- Which of the camps would probably work out BEST for Dan?
- How would you rate Kim's chances for getting the summer job?
- Based on what you know about the Martinez family, which apartment seem to fit its needs BEST?
- Why was moving to Roswell NOT a good decision for Bo?

The lessons in Chapter 4 will help you understand how to answer test questions about everyday texts. You'll read some short everyday texts and answer a few questions about each one. The upcoming lessons also help you organize and synthesize the information in everyday texts in a way that will help you make decisions and draw conclusions.

Selecting Relevant Data

Everyday text often contains the **relevant data**, or information you need, to keep your life running smoothly. Once you select the information you need from an everyday text, you're in a better position to make decisions.

Schedules are a common type of everyday text. Like tables, they contain a great deal of data organized in a logical and easy-to-use format. To find relevant data on a schedule, read the headings for the rows and columns. Make sure you know what they stand for. Then read down the columns and across the rows to find the information you need.

Tips for Success

- Read titles and headings carefully.
- Look for specific pieces of information in the text that will answer the question.
- Combine different pieces of information in a text to choose the correct answer.

Study this schedule. Then use the data in the schedule to answer the question.

GIRLS TUESDAY NIGHT INDOOR SOCCER LEAGUE SCHEDULE

Date Time	2/13	2/27	3/6	3/13	3/20	3/27
5:10 P.M.	1v2	6v8	3v5	3v8	2v3	1v10
6:05 P.M.	3v4	2v5	8v10	6v10	4v5	2v6
7:00 P.M.	5v7	4v9	2v7	2v4	1v6	3v7
7:55 P.M.	6v10	1v3	1v4	7v9	7v8	5v9
8:50 P.M.	8v9	7v10	6v9	1v5	9v10	4v8

Team Numbers			
1	Greenville	6	Livingston
2	Mill Center	7	Wilton
3	New Valley	8	White Mountain
4	Center City	9	Grayfields
5	Riverton	10	Dunmoore

v = against

1. When does the Wilton team play Grayfields?

   A. February 27 at 8:50 P.M.

   B. March 6 at 8:50 P.M.

   C. March 13 at 7:55 P.M.

   D. March 20 at 7:55 P.M.

1. Ⓐ Ⓑ Ⓒ Ⓓ   **Mark your answer choice by filling in the oval.**

✓   **Now check to see whether you chose the correct answer.**

   A. Wilton plays Dunmoore on February 27.

   B. On March 6 at 8:50 P.M., Team 6, Livingston, plays Grayfields.

   C. This is the correct answer. Team 7, Wilton, and Team 9, Grayfields, play at this time.

   D. Wilton plays team 8, White Mountain, on March 20.

Study this schedule for the Alaska Railroad, a summer sightseeing line.

ANCHORAGE — DENALI PARK — FAIRBANKS
Daily Service May 18–Sept.18

City	Northbound	Southbound
Fairbanks	8:30 P.M.	8:30 A.M.
Denali Park	Lv 4:15 P.M.	Ar 12:15 P.M.
Denali Park	Ar 4:00 P.M.	Lv 12:30 P.M.
Talkeetna	11:20 A.M.	4:30 P.M.
Wasilla	9:50 A.M.	6:00 P.M.
Anchorage	8:30 A.M.	8:30 P.M.

Peak Season   June 6–Sept. 4

Value Season   May 18–June 5 & Sept. 5–Sept. 18

One-Way Rail Fare (per person)

Anchorage to Denali Park	$95 peak	$76 value
Anchorage to Fairbanks	$135 peak	$108 value
Denali Park to Fairbanks	$50 peak	$40 value

---

1. Ⓐ Ⓑ Ⓒ Ⓓ
2. Ⓐ Ⓑ Ⓒ Ⓓ
3. Ⓐ Ⓑ Ⓒ Ⓓ
4. Ⓐ Ⓑ Ⓒ Ⓓ

Mark the best answer for questions 1–4.

1. At what time is the train to Fairbanks scheduled to arrive in Denali Park?
   A. 12:15 P.M.
   B. 12:30 P.M.
   C. 4:00 P.M.
   D. 4:15 P.M.

2. If Leah takes the train from Denali Park to Fairbanks on September 10, how much will her ticket cost?
   A. $135
   B. $108
   C. $50
   D. $40

3. The Rayes plan to take a trip from Anchorage to Talkeetna. How long will the trip take?
   A. about 3 hours
   B. about 5 hours
   C. about 6 hours
   D. about 8 hours

4. How much will a round trip from Denali Park to Fairbanks cost a couple if they travel in August?
   A. $50
   B. $80
   C. $160
   D. $200

Lesson 2 Using a Sequence of Data

Being able to follow directions allows you to complete many useful tasks. When reading directions, it is important to determine the order of steps, the **sequence**. Go through the steps quickly at first to get a general idea of what you have to do. Then read them again slowly and carefully.

Since directions are an important part of everyday reading, you usually find them on reading tests. Often you have to identify the sequence—which step comes first, second, or last. Or you have to tell what you should do or watch for at a certain point in the sequence.

Tips for Success
- Look in the text for the specific words and phrases used in a question. The answer will often be nearby.
- Look for words that show time order: *before, after, first, second, next, last, then, finally.*

Read these directions for growing a "pomato" plant. Pay attention to the order of steps you need to follow.

Grafting 1-2-3

Grafting projects require planning ahead. Allow at least 8 weeks from the time you graft the two plants to allow your "pomato" to flower and fruit.

You can grow the potato and tomato plants in separate pots or together in one large pot. When both are about 1 foot (30 cm) high, pull the main stems together. Where they touch, shave each stem with a craft knife just enough to expose the interior tubes. Tie the surfaces together with string; then, press the wax completely around the graft to protect it.

Allow about a week for the graft to take, checking for yellowing or withering on both plants. If the plants look healthy, cut off the top of the potato plant and the bottom of the tomato plant—turning your potato and tomato graft into a single "pomato.". . . . When tomatoes appear above, you can be sure that potatoes grow below!

—Glen Vecchione, *100 Amazing Make-It-Yourself Science Fair Projects*

1. When do you cut off the top of the potato plant?
    A. about a week after grafting
    B. when both are about 1 foot high
    C. as soon as you graft them
    D. at least 8 weeks from the time you graft the two plants

1. Ⓐ Ⓑ Ⓒ Ⓓ **Mark your answer choice by filling in the oval.**

✓ **Now check to see whether you chose the correct answer.**

    A. This is the correct answer. If the plants look healthy a week after the graft, you can cut off the top of the potato and the bottom of the tomato.
    B. You graft the plants when they are about 1-foot high.
    C. After grafting, you have to wait to make sure the graft takes.
    D. Eight weeks after you graft, the plants will flower and fruit.

Test Practice

Read these directions for what to do if someone chokes while eating.

RESPIRATORY EMERGENCIES

- If a person chokes when eating, first assess the blockage, or obstruction.
- If the victim has only a *partial obstruction* of the airway, he or she will be able to speak and cough forcefully, often with a wheezing sound. In such a situation, do not interfere with the victim's attempts to expel the blockage.
- If the victim has a *complete obstruction* of the airway, he or she will be unable to breathe, speak, or cough, and may show distress by grasping at the throat.
- If the victim of a complete obstruction is standing or sitting, use back blows or thrusts.

Back Blows

1. Position yourself at the side of and slightly behind the victim and place one hand high on his chest for support.

2. Lean the victim forward so that his head is at chest level or lower, to utilize the advantages of gravity.

3. Deliver four sharp blows with the heel of your hand as rapidly as possible to the region just below the shoulders.

Thrusts

1. Stand behind the victim and wrap your arms around his waist. Place the thumb side of your fist against the victim's abdomen, slightly above the navel and below the tip of his sternum.

2. Grasp your fist with your other hand and press it into the victim's abdomen with four quick upward thrusts.

---

1. Ⓐ Ⓑ Ⓒ Ⓓ
2. Ⓐ Ⓑ Ⓒ Ⓓ
3. Ⓐ Ⓑ Ⓒ Ⓓ
4. Ⓐ Ⓑ Ⓒ Ⓓ

Mark the best answer for questions 1–4.

1. If a person chokes while eating, what is the first thing you should do?
   - A. Stand behind the victim.
   - B. Encourage the person to sit or lie down.
   - C. Determine whether the blockage is partial or complete.
   - D. Grasp your fist with your other hand and press it into the victim's abdomen.

2. After standing behind a victim to whom you will give back blows, you should next
   - A. place a hand on his chest for support.
   - B. let the victim attempt to expel the blockage.
   - C. lean the victim forward.
   - D. deliver four blows with your hand.

3. How many thrusts should you use to dislodge an obstruction?
   - A. two
   - B. four
   - C. six
   - D. eight

4. A choking victim wheezes while talking. This suggests that he
   - A. will benefit from thrusts.
   - B. should lean forward or lie down.
   - C. has a complete obstruction.
   - D. should attempt to clear the blockage himself.

Lesson 3 Classifying Information

Everyday text can help you make practical choices about what to do. Often you will have to look through a great deal of information to make the right decision. **Classifying information** involves looking through a text and organizing the information in it in order to make a choice or reach a logical conclusion.

Tips for Success
- Keep in mind the decision that has to be made.
- Go through all the possibilities. Check off any that don't work.
- If there is more than one solution, choose the one that makes the best sense.

Read this page from a wilderness survival fieldbook, which describes types of winter camp shelters.

TENTS A tent provides the least insulation of any winter shelter. While it goes up fast, tents flap unpleasantly in high winds and snow can drift over them.

SNOW DOMES In flat terrain where the snow isn't too deep, a snow dome makes an ideal shelter. Basically a huge mound of snow that has been shoveled up and hollowed out, the dome takes just a few hours to build and is ideal in cold temperatures.

SNOW CAVES Similar to domes, snow caves are dug into the deep drifts or steep snow slopes found in hilly or forested terrain. Easier to make than a dome, the aerodynamically-sound snow cave provides perfect protection in the worst storms.

IGLOO Building a proper igloo takes time and practice, but the finished product is the most comfortable snow structure and ideal when camping for a week or more at a site. The best snow to use is on open, windswept slopes. Temperatures must be no more than 25°F at day (10°F at night) for the snow to be firm enough.

1. Olga and Mei are winter camping for two days. The temperature is 15°F, the wind is blowing hard, and it might snow. They're hiking on an open plain covered by six inches of snow. The sun will set in about four hours. Although they have a tent, the teens would like to try a snow shelter. The BEST decision for them to make is to

A. use their tent.

B. build a snow cave.

C. build a snow dome.

D. build an igloo.

 1. Ⓐ Ⓑ Ⓒ Ⓓ **Mark your answer choice by filling in the oval.**

 Now check to see whether you chose the correct answer.

A. A snow shelter would be more comfortable and the girls want to try it.

B. The terrain isn't right for a snow cave.

C. This is the correct answer. Considering the snow conditions and terrain, this is the best choice.

D. Olga and Mei don't have time to build or benefit from an igloo.

Read these descriptions of swimming strokes that appear in the *Boy Scout Fieldbook.*

CRAWL Combining continuous arm motion with a strong flutter kick, the crawl is the fastest of the basic swimming strokes. It also is the most tiring. The crawl will get you quickly away from danger, pull you to a nearby shore, or help you win a race. However, if you have far to swim or must be in the water a long time, choose a stroke that will not so easily exhaust you.

BREASTSTROKE The breaststroke is an easy, energy-saving way to swim. You extend your arms in front of you, sweep them out until they are almost even with your shoulders, return them to the starting point, glide a moment, then repeat the motion. Meanwhile, use your legs to push yourself along with a whip kick or breaststroke kick . . . . In rescue situations, you can use the breaststroke to keep your head high to see what you're doing as you approach a struggling swimmer.

ELEMENTARY BACKSTROKE Similar to a breaststroke done on your back, the elementary backstroke allows you to rest as you glide. You'll be able to cover long distances without expending too much energy, making this one of the most important survival strokes. Take a breath of air as you end each stroke so that you'll have full lungs to make you more buoyant while you glide, but don't glide too long. Start your next stroke before you stop moving from the force of the last one.

SIDESTROKE The sidestroke depends for propulsion on a scissors kick that uses the power of leg muscles conditioned by walking and running. Paired with a smooth arm motion, the kick gives you a long glide between strokes, and the position of your head makes breathing easy. Like the elementary backstroke, it is good for long survival swims.

TRUDGEN The trudgen stroke is a combination stroke that employs the arm motion of the crawl and the scissors kick of the sidestroke. It's fast and efficient over short distances and for lifesaving in rough water.

---

1. Ⓐ Ⓑ Ⓒ Ⓓ
2. Ⓐ Ⓑ Ⓒ Ⓓ
3. Ⓐ Ⓑ Ⓒ Ⓓ
4. Ⓐ Ⓑ Ⓒ Ⓓ

Mark the best answer for questions 1–4.

1. Cal's rowboat has sunk, and he must swim a mile to shore. He's not a powerful swimmer. Which stroke(s) should he use?
   A. the crawl
   B. the elementary backstroke
   C. the crawl and the breaststroke
   D. the trudgen

2. Diana has to rescue a child in rough water. Which stroke should she use?
   A. the elementary backstroke
   B. the crawl
   C. the sidestroke
   D. the trudgen

3. While swimming in a pond, Ray sees a poisonous water snake drop from a branch into the water near him. To exit the area, Ray should use
   A. the crawl.
   B. the elementary backstroke.
   C. the sidestroke.
   D. the breaststroke.

4. Millie is only familiar with the flutter and scissors kicks. Which would she NOT be able to swim?
   A. the crawl
   B. the sidestroke
   C. the breaststroke
   D. the trudgen

Synthesizing Information

Sometimes you will have to use information from more than one everyday text to make a decision. **Synthesizing information** is combining information from different sources. By synthesizing information, you can make a well-informed decision or judgment.

Tips for Success
- Study the texts carefully.
- Keep in mind what you're trying to decide.
- Go through all the possibilities.

Here are tables showing the fitness scale for boys and girls.

Norms by Age for the 1-mile Walk/Run for Boys (in minutes and seconds)

PERCENTILE	10	11	12	13	14	15	16	17	18
99	6:55	6:21	6:21	5:59	5:43	5:40	5:31	5:14	5:33
90	8:13	7:25	7:13	6:48	6:27	6:23	6:13	6:08	6:10
80	8:35	7:52	7:41	7:07	6:58	6:43	6:31	6:31	6:33
75	8:48	8:02	7:53	7:14	7:08	6:52	6:39	6:40	6:42
70	9:02	8:12	8:03	7:24	7:18	7:00	6:50	6:46	6:57
60	9:26	8:38	8:23	6:46	7:34	7:13	7:07	7:10	7:15
50	9:52	9:03	8:48	8:04	7:51	7:30	7:27	7:31	7:35

Norms by Age for the 1-mile Walk/Run for Girls (in minutes and seconds)

PERCENTILE	10	11	12	13	14	15	16	17	18
99	7:55	7:14	7:20	7:08	7:01	6:59	7:03	6:52	6:58
90	9:09	8:45	8:34	8:27	8:11	8:23	8:28	8:20	8:22
80	9:56	9:35	9:30	9:13	8:49	9:04	9:06	9:10	9:27
75	10:09	9:56	9:52	9:30	9:16	9:28	9:25	9:26	9:31
70	10:27	10:10	10:05	9:48	9:31	9:49	9:41	9:41	9:36
60	10:51	10:35	10:32	10:22	10:04	10:20	10:15	10:16	10:08
50	11:14	11:15	10:58	10:52	10:32	10:46	10:34	10:34	10:51

Source: The National Children and Youth Fitness Study (NCYFS)

1. Ellen and her twin brother Jack are 14. For a fitness test at school, Ellen completes the 1-mile walk/run in 8 minutes and 4 seconds. Jack completes it in 7 minutes and 3 seconds. Who is at or above the 90th percentile?

   A. both Jack and Ellen

   B. neither Jack nor Ellen

   C. only Jack

   D. only Ellen

1. Ⓐ Ⓑ Ⓒ Ⓓ   **Mark your answer choice by filling in the oval.**

✔ **Now check to see whether you chose the correct answer.**

   A. The 90th percentile norm for 14-year-old boys is 6:27.

   B. The 90th percentile norm for 14-year-old girls is 8:11.

   C. Look at the table again and compare Jack's time with that listed for a 14-year-old boy at the 90th percentile.

   D. This is the correct answer. Only Ellen is at the 90th percentile.

Use the tables to answer the questions below.

The Health-Related Fitness Test Standards for Girls

Age	Sit and Reach (inches)	Sit-ups (number)	Pull-ups (number)	Flexed Arm Hang (seconds)
10	10.0	30	1	8
11	10.0	30	1	8
12	10.0	30	1	8
13	10.0	30	1	12
14	10.0	35	1	12
15	10.0	35	1	12
16	10.0	35	1	12
16+	10.0	35	1	12

The Health-Related Fitness Test Standards for Boys

Age	Sit and Reach (inches)	Sit-ups (number)	Pull-ups (number)	Flexed Arm Hang (seconds)
10	10.0	30	1	10
11	10.0	30	1	10
12	10.0	35	1	10
13	10.0	35	2	10
14	10.0	40	3	15
15	10.0	40	5	25
16	10.0	40	5	25
16+	10.0	40	5	25

Source: The National Children and Youth Fitness Study (NCYFS)

1. Ⓐ Ⓑ Ⓒ Ⓓ
2. Ⓐ Ⓑ Ⓒ Ⓓ
3. Ⓐ Ⓑ Ⓒ Ⓓ
4. Ⓐ Ⓑ Ⓒ Ⓓ

Mark the best answer for questions 1–4.

1. Which health-related fitness test does NOT change for either boys or girls?

   A. sit and reach

   B. sit-ups

   C. pull-ups

   D. flexed arm hang

2. Based on the tables, which is true?

   A. Physically-fit boys and girls can do at least one pull-up until age 16.

   B. At 13, physically-fit girls have to do the flexed arm hang longer than boys.

   C. At age 12, physically-fit boys and girls can do 30 sit-ups.

   D. As boys and girls grow older, they do not need to increase the number of pull-ups they can do.

3. Between the ages of 11 and 13, the number of sit-ups that a physically-fit child should be able to perform

   A. stays the same for boys and girls.

   B. increases by 5 for girls and boys.

   C. increases by 5 for girls.

   D. increases by 5 for boys.

4. Fifteen-year-old Maria can do 30 sit-ups, 2 pull-ups, and hang on a flexed arm for 13 seconds. In which skill is she *below* normal for physical fitness?

   A. sit and reach

   B. sit-ups

   C. pull-ups

   D. flexed arm hang

Use these samples of everyday text to practice the skills you've learned in this chapter. Read the texts and answer the questions. Mark your answer choices by filling in the ovals.

Use this section from a performance schedule for a summer theater company to answer questions 1–2.

SCHEDULE OF PERFORMANCE—JUNE

Tuesday	Wednesday	Thursday	Friday	Saturday	Sunday
2	3	4 8:00 EYES W*	5 8:00 EYES W*	6 3:30 EYES W* 8:00 EYES W°	7 3:30 EYES W
9	10	11 8:00 EYES W	12 8:00 EYES W 8:30 ALL S*	13 3:30 ALL S* 3:30 EYES W 8:00 EYES W	14 3:30 ALL S* 3:30 EYES W
16	17	18 8:00 EYES W 8:30 ALL S*	19 8:00 EYES W 8:30 ALL S*	20 3:30 SHREW S* 3:30 EYES W 8:00 EYES W 8:30 ALL S°	21 3:30 SHREW S* 3:30 EYES W 8:30 ALL S
23 LEAR S*	24 3:30 SHREW S* 8:30 LEAR S°	25 8:00 SHREW S* 8:30 LEAR S	26 8:00 EYES W 8:30 ALL S	27 3:30 LEAR S 5:30 GALA M 8:00 EYES W 8:30 SHREW S*	28 3:30 LEAR S• 8:00 EYES W 8:30 ALL S

ABBREVIATIONS AND SYMBOLS

Private Eyes	EYES	M	Mainstage	*	preview
All's Well That Ends Well	ALL	S	Stables Theatre	o	opening
Taming of the Shrew	SHREW	W	Wharton Theatre	•	closing
Lear Project	LEAR	O	Oxford Court Theatre		
Gala Celebration	GALA				

1. Ⓐ Ⓑ Ⓒ Ⓓ
2. Ⓐ Ⓑ Ⓒ Ⓓ

SELECT RELEVANT DATA

1. In June, how many performances of *Lear Project* will there be, including previews?

A. three

B. four

C. five

D. six

SELECT RELEVANT DATA

2. Tickets for previews of shows are discounted 10%. The last date to take advantage of the discounted price for *All's Well That Ends Well* is

A. June 13.

B. June 19.

C. June 20.

D. June 26.

Use these directions to answer questions 3–6.

3. Ⓐ Ⓑ Ⓒ Ⓓ
4. Ⓐ Ⓑ Ⓒ Ⓓ
5. Ⓐ Ⓑ Ⓒ Ⓓ
6. Ⓐ Ⓑ Ⓒ Ⓓ

To Charge the 6.0V Rechargeable NiCd (Nickel-Cadmium) Battery Pack

1. Plug the wall pack charger into standard 110/220 volt outlet.
2. Click the battery pack into the charger. Check that the battery pack is secure in charger.
3. Charge the battery pack for 5 1/2 hours the first two times you charge battery. Subsequent charges will require only 4 hours.
4. To disconnect the battery pack, push the red button on the side of the charger and simultaneously slide the battery pack back out.
5. After charging for 4 or more hours, the battery will feel warm. This condition is normal for fully charged batteries.
6. Unlike alkaline batteries, where the power loss is gradual, a NiCd battery will suddenly lose much of its power. This indicates it is time to recharge.
7. After use, the battery pack will be hot! Wait at least 20 minutes before recharging so the battery can cool. Recharging a warm or hot battery pack will greatly reduce the number of times it can be recharged.
8. If the battery pack and connector are wet, dry thoroughly before recharging.
9. Never attempt to recharge a battery pack that shows leakage or corrosion.

USE SEQUENCE OF DATA

3. According to the directions, when should the battery pack be charged for 5 1/2 hours?

   A. the first time only

   B. the first two times

   C. the first three times

   D. every time

USE SEQUENCE OF DATA

4. What will happen if you attempt to recharge a warm or hot battery?

   A. The battery will not recharge and will have to be replaced.

   B. The battery pack will show gradual leakage or corrosion.

   C. The battery might explode because of overheating.

   D. The number of times the battery can be recharged will be greatly reduced.

USE SEQUENCE OF DATA

5. What should you do before you click the battery pack into the charger?

   A. Push the red button to disconnect the battery.

   B. Plug in the wall pack charger.

   C. Wait 20 minutes to make sure the battery is secure.

   D. Unplug the power pack.

SELECT RELEVANT DATA

6. How are nickel-cadmium batteries different from alkaline batteries?

   A. Alkaline batteries cannot be recharged.

   B. Nickel-cadmium batteries get hot when used.

   C. Alkaline batteries do not leak or show corrosion.

   D. Nickel-cadmium batteries lose their power suddenly.

Use this page from a first-aid manual to answer questions 7–9.

SNAKEBITES

If you are bitten by a snake, it is important to know whether or not the snake is poisonous. There are four major kinds of poisonous snakes in the United States: rattlesnakes, copperheads. cottonmouths, and coral snakes. You should become familiar with the appearance of these snakes. Try to capture and kill the snake that bit you, without damaging the head, or at least be able to describe the snake.

Poisonous Snakes The rattlesnake, copperhead, and cottonmouth all have slitlike eyes with poison sacs behind them. They also have long fangs. The coral snake has rounded eyes, but has fangs and poison sacs like the other poisonous snakes.

Rattlesnakes have a characteristic rattle on the end of their tails. Cottonmouths, also called water moccasins, have a white lining in their mouths, for which they are named. A coral snake has red, yellow, and black rings and a black nose.

Treating Snakebites The instructions below do not apply if the person is bitten by a coral snake. In such cases, the person should be immobilized and medical help obtained immediately. In the case of any snakebite, keep the bitten area below the person's heart, if possible.

1. First call 911 or your emergency number. If the bite is on the arm or leg, place a light constricting band 2 in to 4 in (5 cm to 10 cm) above the bite toward the body. Do not cut off circulation. Leave the band on until medical help arrives. Wash the bite area with soap and water. Immobilize the area. Do not use ice or cold compresses.

2. Keep the person as quiet as possible. This will help to slow the circulation, which will, in turn, help stop the venom from spreading. Do not let the person walk unless absolutely necessary and, if so, then very slowly. Do not attempt to suck out the venom.

CLASSIFY

7. Which detail about coral snakes will NOT help you distinguish them from cottonmouths?

   A. A coral snake has red and yellow rings.

   B. A coral snake has a black nose.

   C. A coral snake has poison sacs.

   D. A coral snake has round eyes.

CLASSIFY

8. Based on the passage, which seems to have the most dangerous bite?

   A. rattlesnakes

   B. copperheads

   C. coral snakes

   D. cottonmouths

CLASSIFY

9. While waiting for emergency help, what should you do for someone bitten on the back by a rattlesnake?

   A. Use a light constricting band to slow circulation.

   B. Suck out the poison.

   C. Place ice on the bite.

   D. Wash the bite with soapy water.

Use these tips for getting bluebirds to nest in your area to answer questions 10–11.

EASTERN BLUEBIRDS

Number of Eggs Laid
in Clutch: 3–6
Days to Hatch: 13–16
Days Young in Nest: 15–16

Number of Broods
Each Year: 2, sometimes 3
Lifespan: 3 to 7 years

Eastern bluebirds range across eastern North America and west to the Rockies. Their grassy nests are built in the natural cavity of a tree or wooden fence post, or in a woodpecker hole.

Bluebird Nest Boxes Make the round entrance hole of your bluebird nest boxes exactly 1 1/2 inches in diameter. The slightly larger starling, the bluebird's strongest competitor for nesting places, cannot get into a bird box with an entrance hole this size. Build the box 5 inches square, inside dimensions, and 8 inches deep from top of the floor to the inside bottom of the roof. Bore the 1 1/2-inch entrance hole 6 inches above the floor of the box.

Unwanted Visitors To keep house (or "English") sparrows out of bluebird houses, place the bluebird house on a *post no higher than five feet above the ground.* House sparrows usually will not nest this close to the ground. If the house sparrows persist in nesting in the low-placed bluebird houses, cut a *rectangular* entrance hole in the box, 1 1/2 inches high and only *1 1/4 inches* wide. This will allow the slenderer bluebird to get in, but will usually keep out the pudgier sparrow.

Rule of Thumb Mount your bluebird boxes about 4 feet above the ground, facing a quiet road, but away from pastures where grazing animals might damage them.

Clean Your Nest Boxes Many bluebirds will not nest in a box that has old nesting material in it. After each nesting is over and the young birds have left the box, sweep out the old nesting material.

SYNTHESIZE

10. What is the maximum number of young that a pair of bluebirds nesting in a box could produce during the course of one spring and summer?

   A. 9

   B. 12

   C. 18

   D. 24

SYNTHESIZE

11. Sandy mounted a bluebird box on the roof of the family garage. No bluebirds have taken up residence, however. This is PROBABLY because

   A. the entrance hole is too small.

   B. the box is too high.

   C. the box has not been cleaned.

   D. there isn't a ready supply of insects for the bluebirds to eat.

12. Describe how you would solve this problem: House sparrows nested in your bluebird box instead of bluebirds.

This Practice Test includes reading passages that represent the four types of text you studied in this book—narrative, informational, persuasive, and everyday. As you take the test, keep in mind what you have learned. The skills you gained will help you read the passages effectively, understand the questions being asked, and answer them successfully.

Read the following short story by Sean O'Faolain about an unusual occurrence in a young girl's summer. Then answer the questions. Mark your answer choices on the answer sheet provided.

The Trout

1. One of the first places Julia always ran to when they arrived in G__ was The Dark Walk. It is a laurel walk, very old; almost gone wild; a lofty midnight tunnel of smooth, sinewy branches. Underfoot the tough brown leaves are never dry enough to crackle: there is always a suggestion of damp and cool trickle.

2. She raced right into it. For the first few yards she always had the memory of the sun behind her, then she felt the dusk closing swiftly down on her so that she screamed with pleasure and raced on to reach the light at the far end; and it was always just a little too long in coming so that she emerged gasping, clasping her hands, laughing, drinking in the sun. When she was filled with the heat and glare she would turn and consider the ordeal again.

3. This year she had the extra joy of showing it to her small brother, and of terrifying him as well as herself. And for him the fear lasted longer because his legs were so short and she had gone out at the far end while he was still screaming and racing.

4. When they had done this many times they came back to the house to tell everybody that they had done it. He boasted. She mocked. They squabbled.

5. "Cry babby!"

6. "You were afraid yourself, so there!"

7. "I won't take you any more."

8. "You're a big pig."

9. "I hate you."

10. Tears were threatening, so somebody said, "Did you see the well?" She opened her eyes at that and held up her long lovely neck suspiciously and decided to be incredulous. She was twelve and at that age little girls are beginning to suspect most stories: they have already found out too many, from Santa Claus to the stork. How could there be a well! In The Dark Walk? That she had visited year after year? Haughtily she said, "Nonsense."

11. But she went back, pretending to be going somewhere else, and she found a hole scooped in the rock at the side of the walk, choked with damp leaves, so shrouded by ferns that she uncovered it only after much searching. At the back of this little cavern there was about a quart of water. In the water she suddenly perceived a panting trout. She rushed for Stephen and dragged him to see, and they were both so excited that

they were no longer afraid of the darkness as they hunched down and peered in at the fish panting in his tiny prison, his silver stomach going up and down like an engine.

12. Nobody knew how the trout got there. Even old Martin in the kitchen garden laughed and refused to believe . . . .

13. Her mother suggested that a bird had carried the spawn. Her father thought that in the winter a small streamlet might have carried it down there as a baby, and it had been safe until the summer came and the water began to dry up. She said, "I see," and went back to look again and consider the matter in private. Her brother remained behind, wanting to hear the whole story of the trout, not really interested in the actual trout but much interested in the story which his mummy began to make up for him on the lines of, "So one day Daddy Trout and Mammy Trout. . ." When he retailed it to her, she said, "Pooh."

14. It troubled her that the trout was always in the same position; he had no room to turn; all the time the silver belly went up and down; otherwise he was motionless. She wondered what he ate, and in between visits to Joey Pony and the boat, and a bathe to get cool, she thought of his hunger. She brought him down bits of dough; once she brought him a worm. He ignored the food. He just went on panting. Hunched over him she thought how all the winter, while she was at school, he had been in there. All the winter, in The Dark Walk, all day, all night, floating around alone. She drew the leaf of her hat down around her ears and chin and stared. She was still thinking of it as she lay in bed.

15. It was late June, the longest day of the year. The sun had sat still for a week, burning up the world. Although it was after ten o'clock it was still bright and still hot. She lay on her back under a single sheet, with her long legs spread, trying to keep cool. She could see the D of the moon through the fir tree—they slept on the ground floor. Before they went to bed her mummy had told Stephen the story of the trout again, and she, in her bed, had resolutely presented her back to them and read her book. But she had kept one ear cocked.

16. "And so, in the end, this naughty fish who would not stay at home got bigger and bigger and bigger, and the water got smaller and smaller. . . ."

17. Passionately she had whirled and cried, "Mummy, don't make it a horrible old moral story!" Her mummy had brought in a fairy godmother then, who sent lots of rain, and filled the well, and a stream poured out and the trout floated away down to the river below. Staring at the moon she knew that there are no such things as fairy godmothers and that the trout, down in The Dark Walk, was panting like an engine. She heard somebody unwind a fishing reel. Would the *beasts* fish him out?

18. She sat up. Stephen was a hot lump of sleep, lazy thing. The Dark Walk would be full of little scraps of moon. She leaped up and looked out the window, and somehow it was not so lightsome now that she saw the dim mountains far away and the black firs against the breathing land and heard a dog say *bark-bark*. Quietly, she lifted the **ewer** of water and climbed out the window and scuttled along the cool but cruel gravel down to the maw of the tunnel. Something alive rustled inside there. She raced in, and up and down she raced, and flurried, and cried aloud,

"Oh, gosh, I can't find it," and then at last she did. Kneeling down in the damp she put her hand into the slimy hole. When the body lashed they were both mad with fright. But she gripped him and shoved him into the ewer and raced, with her teeth ground, out to the other end of the tunnel and down the steep paths to the river's edge.

19. All the time she could feel him lashing his tail against the side of the ewer. She was afraid he would jump right out. The gravel cut into her soles until she came to the cool ooze of the river's bank where the moon mice on the water crept into her feet. She poured out, watching until he plopped. For a second he was visible in the water. She hoped he was not dizzy. Then all she saw was the glimmer of the moon in the silent-flowing river, the dark firs, the dim mountains, and the radiant pointed face laughing down at her out of the empty sky.

20. She scuttled up the hill, in the window, plonked down the ewer, and flew through the air like a bird into bed. The dog said *bark-bark*. She heard the fishing reel whirring. She hugged herself and giggled. Like a river of joy her holiday spread before her.

21. In the morning, Stephen rushed to her, shouting that "he" was gone, and asking "where" and "how." Lifting her nose in the air she said superciliously, "Fairy godmother, I suppose?" and strolled away patting the palms of her hands.

---

1. The place named G— in the story seems to be
   A. a children's country summer camp.
   B. a vacation house in the country.
   C. a day camp in a city park.
   D. a remote forest.

2. Which words BEST describe Julia?
   A. irritable and shy
   B. independent and suspicious
   C. nervous and selfish
   D. fanciful and spoiled

3. According to the story,
   A. a bird carried the trout to the well.
   B. a river washed the trout into the well.
   C. Martin put the trout in the well.
   D. no one knew how the trout got there.

4. The description of the sun at the beginning of paragraph 15 is
   A. a simile.
   B. a metaphor.
   C. personification.
   D. hyperbole.

5. The setting inside The Dark Walk creates a mood of
   A. joy and optimism.
   B. restlessness and suspicion.
   C. mystery and awe.
   D. ugliness and decay.

6. What seemed to trouble Julia MOST about the trout?
   A. She didn't know how it got there.
   B. It was alone and could not move.
   C. She had to feed it.
   D. Martin threatened to kill and eat it.

7. What does Julia resent most about her mother's telling the trout story?

   A. Her mother has never even gone to see the trout.

   B. Julia considers herself too old to have to listen to bedtime stories.

   C. Her mother's story is too realistic.

   D. The story does not mention that Julia was first to find the trout.

8. Why might the last scene occur on the longest day of the year?

   A. The long day stresses how bored and unhappy Julia has become.

   B. The long day symbolizes how long the trout has been out of water.

   C. The heat of the day stresses the tension Julia is feeling.

   D. The brutally hot day contrasts with the upbeat story Julia's mother tells.

9. The ewer that Julia carries at the end of the story is

   A. a glass.

   B. a soda bottle.

   C. a pitcher.

   D. a basket.

10. When the fish's panting is compared to an engine in paragraph 17, the author is using

    A. a simile.

    B. a metaphor.

    C. personification.

    D. hyperbole.

11. Julia's action at the end of the story shows her to be

    A. deceptive.

    B. emotional.

    C. inconsistent.

    D. decisive.

12. At the end of the story, Julia decides

    A. to avoid The Dark Walk in the future.

    B. to write her own story about the trout.

    C. to release the trout into the river.

    D. to bring the trout to Martin.

13. Which message does the author probably NOT intend to express?

    A. New life and hope often lie hidden in dark places.

    B. Adults have a deeper understanding of nature than children.

    C. We all need to find space to develop our full potential.

    D. It's important to appreciate the mysteries of life.

14. Why do you think Julia identified so closely with the trout? What do you think her action at the end of the story might represent?

_____

_____

_____

STOP

45 Read the following passage about old Russia from a social studies textbook and answer the questions. Mark your answer choices on the answer sheet provided.

Kievan Russia

1. The ancestors of today's Russian people were the East Slavs. The origins of the East Slavs and the precise time they first settled on the Eurasian Plain are not known. These origins have been obscured by many waves of invasion and migration, and by the passage of more than a thousand years. But we do know that by the A.D. 800s the East Slavs had begun to develop their civilization there. During the 900s, the first Russian state grew along the rivers that form a natural waterway between the Baltic Sea and the Black Sea. The ruling dynasty of this state was a group of powerful merchant warriors from Scandinavia, the Vikings, who gradually merged with the native Slavs. The term *Rus* came to be used for this combination of Scandinavians and Slavs.

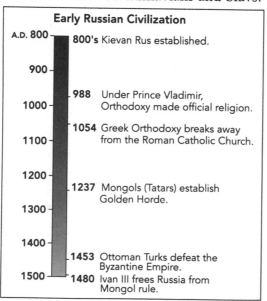

Early Russian Civilization

A.D. 800 — **800's** Kievan Rus established.

900 —

1000 — **988** Under Prince Vladimir, Orthodoxy made official religion.

1100 — **1054** Greek Orthodoxy breaks away from the Roman Catholic Church.

1200 —

1300 — **1237** Mongols (Tatars) establish Golden Horde.

1400 —

1500 — **1453** Ottoman Turks defeat the Byzantine Empire.
1480 Ivan III frees Russia from Mongol rule.

2. The center of the first Russian state was Kiev, a city in what today is Ukraine, on the lower reaches of the Dnieper River. Kiev was not a unified nation like the Russian Empire or the Soviet Union. It was a loose federation of city-states, each one controlled by a prince of the ruling family. Kievan Russia compared favorably with its neighboring states in Europe. Its economy was based on the small-scale agriculture of its mostly free peasants. Nonetheless, much of Kievan Russia's prosperity and character came from trade.

3. The river network controlled by the Kievans was a major trade route linking Europe to the Middle East and beyond. The Kievan rulers encouraged and engaged in this trade. Their major trading partner, the richest and most culturally advanced of Russia's neighbors, was the Byzantine Empire to the south. This empire's capital, Constantinople, was the most magnificent city in the Western world. Every year hundreds of boats sailed down the Dnieper to the Black Sea and then on to Constantinople. There they unloaded their furs, wax, honey, grain, slaves, and forest products, exchanging them for wines, perfumes, and other Byzantine luxuries.

4. In this way Byzantine culture, crafts, and religion were brought into Russia. The movement and borrowing of ideas, beliefs, objects, and customs between regions is called *cultural diffusion*. The interdependence between Kievan Russia and the Byzantine Empire led to a cultural diffusion that helped shape the modern nation-state of Russia.

5. The Byzantine religion was Greek Orthodox Christianity. When Kiev's Prince Vladimir converted to it in 988, it became the official religion of his realm. This event is one of the key events in Russian history. Greek Orthodoxy became the established religion in Russia, while the dominant religion in most of central and western Europe was Roman Catholicism. The head of the Greek Orthodox Church was the Patriarch of Constantinople. He appointed the metropolitan (chief bishop) of Kiev, the religious leader of that city. The metropolitan was usually a Greek, not a Russian, although many of the lower clergy were Russian. In 1054, the Greek Orthodox Church broke away from the Roman Catholic Church because of a disagreement over the authority of the Pope in Rome. This helped to separate Russia from Western Europe.

THE CYRILLIC ALPHABET			
Cyrillic	**Pronunciation**	**Cyrillic**	**Pronunciation**
А (a)	as in father	С (s)	as in sign
Б (b)	as in bit	Т (t)	as in ten
В (v)	as in vote	У (u)	as in pool
Г (g)	as in goat	Ф (f)	as in fit
Д (d)	as in dog	Х (kh)	as in Bach
Е (e)	as in yes		in German
Ё (e)	as in yoke	Ц (ts)	as in cats
Ж (zh)	as in azure	Ч (ch)	as in cheer
З (z)	as in zero	Ш (sh)	as in shop
И (i)	as in machine	Щ (shch)	as in cash
Й (i)	as in boy		check
К (k)	as in kit	Ъ	hard sign, no
Л (l)	as in let		pronunciation
М (m)	as in map	Ы (y)	as in shrill
Н (n)	as in not	Ь	soft sign, no
О (o)	as in note		pronunciation
П (p)	as in pat	Э (e)	as in bed
Р (r)	as in ravioli	Ю (iu)	as in cute
	(rolled r)	Я (ya)	as in yard

6. This division was widened by another event. During the 800s, the missionary work of two monks, Cyril and Methodius, had led to the adoption of the newly devised Cyrillic alphabet for writing Russian. The Cyrillic alphabet uses letters based on Greek ones. (See table above.) In contrast, Western Europe used (and still uses) the Latin alphabet. The major result of embracing the Greek Orthodox religion and the Cyrillic alphabet was that much of the learning and intellectual developments of Western Europe were inaccessible to educated Russians.

7. Still, in the 1000s Kiev was the largest city in Eastern Europe and was as impressive in many ways as the major cities of Western Europe. With its many beautiful churches, Kiev compared well with the glorious city of Constantinople. Moreover, Kiev was merely one of several well-developed Russian cities. Novgorod was a major center of trade . . . . Other vibrant cities

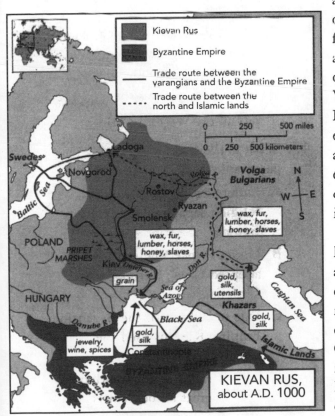

Kievan Rus
Byzantine Empire
Trade route between the varangians and the Byzantine Empire
Trade route between the north and Islamic lands

KIEVAN RUS, about A.D. 1000

were Rostov and Ryazan. These Russian cities all had citizen councils of self-government called *veches*, which shared power with the assemblies of nobles and the princes. Literature, architecture, and art flourished, much of it related to religious themes. A rich secular literature also developed . . . .

8. Kiev's achievements, however, were not enough to prevent its decline. Its strength was sapped by numerous wars and power struggles among its jealous princes. Its economic strength was undermined when the river trade route between Europe and the Middle East was replaced by a more direct route that was opened up by Italian merchants via the Mediterranean Sea. Finally, even at its height, Kiev was under constant pressure from nomadic peoples moving westward out of the Asian heartland. In the 1200s, with Kievan Russia already weakened, the Mongols—by far the most powerful of these nomads—burst out of Asia. In 1223, they gave Russia a brief but terrible taste of their power. They crushed a Russian army in a battle on the Kalka River near the Sea of Azov. Then, to Russia's relief, the Mongols returned home because their leader had died and a successor had to be chosen. Fourteen years later they returned. This time Russia received no relief. The Mongols—or Tatars, as the Russians called them—devastated the land. Kiev and most of Russia's other major cities were destroyed. In Ryazan, the first city to fall, it was said that "not an eye was left open to weep for those that were closed . . . ." After enslaving perhaps 10 percent of Russia's population . . . and carrying off whatever valuables they could, the Tatars established a state called the Golden Horde on the southern steppe . . . . From there they controlled Russia with efficiency and brutality for almost 250 years.

15. What did the author MOST want to accomplish by writing this passage?

   A. to show the influence of Greek Orthodoxy on Russia

   B. to explain the causes for the downfall of Kievan Rus

   C. to trace the early history of the Russian state

   D. to provide an overview of medieval Russian culture

16. What is the main idea of paragraph 3?

   A. Of all of Russia's neighbors, the Byzantine Empire was the most advanced.

   B. The Kievans traded their raw materials for luxuries from the Byzantine Empire.

   C. The Kievans carried on a lively trade with the Byzantine Empire and beyond.

   D. Constantinople was the grandest city in the Western world.

17. What is the main idea of paragraphs 5–6?

   A. Differences in language and religion separated Russia from Europe.

   B. Under Prince Vladimir, Russia adopted Greek Orthodox Christianity.

   C. Due to links with the Byzantine Empire, Kievans used the Cyrillic alphabet.

   D. The Patriarch in Constantinople exerted great influence over Kievan Russia.

18. Which detail does NOT support the main idea in paragraph 8?

A. power struggles among Kievan princes

B. the opening of trade routes across the Mediterranean Sea

C. conflict over the authority of the Roman Catholic church

D. pressure from nomadic peoples to the west

19. According to the timeline on p.74, how long did Kievan Russia practice Greek Orthodoxy before the break with the Roman Catholic Church?

A. about 25 years

B. about 65 years

C. about 125 years

D. about 165 years

20. Which conclusion follows MOST closely from the table on p.75?

A. Cyrillic letters correspond almost exactly to their Roman equivalents.

B. The Cyrillic alphabet expresses fewer sounds than the Roman alphabet.

C. Some Cyrillic letters express a blend of sounds that requires two Roman letters.

D. The Cyrillic alphabet is easier to learn and use than the Roman alphabet.

21. Based on the map on p.75, about how many miles would a boat from Kiev travel down the Dnieper River to reach the Black Sea?

A. about 300 miles

B. about 400 miles

C. about 500 miles

D. about 600 miles

22. Which pages listed in the part of the index shown below might tell about the Mongol invasion of Kievan Russia?

> *taiga,* 13–14
> Tajikistan, 190, 195, 203–205
> *Tale of the Host of Igor, The*
>   187, 189
> Taras Bulba, 199, 201
> Tatars, 69–75
> Tien Shan Mountains, 6

A. 13–14

B. 69–75

C. 190, 195, 203–205

D. 199, 201

23. Which volume and page of the encyclopedia listed below would most likely tell about everyday life in Kievan Russia?

> Kiev [capital of Ukraine] K:124
>   Architecture (history) A:366
>   Russia (the Kievan State) R:523
>   Russian Orthodoxy R:545

A. Volume K, page 124

B. Volume A, page 366

C. Volume R, page 523

D. Volume R, page 545

24. Using the map on p. 75, describe a typical Kievan trading expedition, focusing on the route taken and the goods traded.

_____

_____

_____

Read the essay. Then use the skills you have practiced in Chapter 3 to answer the questions. Mark your answer choices on the answer sheet provided.

The Old Block
by Anna Quindlen

Pulitzer Prize–winning author Anna Quindlen explored timely issues in a weekly column in The New York Times.

1. The block on which my father grew up half a century ago is a truncated little street that leads nowhere. If it were a foot or two narrower, the map makers might have called it an alley. The houses are identical two-story attached brick buildings with bay windows on the top floor, an overobvious attempt at grandeur.

2. In this quiet backwater in the southwestern part of the city the children of Irish-Catholic families played in the late afternoons after they had changed from their parochial school uniforms. A police officer walked by twice a day, talking to the people he knew so well.

3. My father remembers that in one fifteen-minute span when he was eight years old he was hit by four people to whom he was not related: the cop; the neighbor whose window he drew upon with spit; the priest who saw him messing with a statue; and the nun who saw the priest whack him and wanted to second the emotion. So he grew.

4. Today the kids on the block are black. The house where the seven Quindlen children were raised, the boys packed two to a bed, has long been empty. The small setback porch is still covered with debris from the fire that gutted the building several years ago. There is plywood nailed over the glassless windows and the doorless doorway.

5. This was a prosperous neighborhood, a way station to something better. Today it is a poor one, a dead end. Charred interiors are common. So are crime, drugs, and a sense of going nowhere.

6. Since L.A. burst into flames we have cast a net of blame in our search for those who abandoned America's cities.

7. The answer is simple. We did. Over my lifetime, prosperity in America has been measured in moving vans, backyards, and the self-congratulatory remark "I can't remember the last time I went to the city." America became a circle of suburbs surrounding an increasingly grim urban core.

8. In the beginning there was a **synergy** between the two; we took the train to the city to work and shop, then fled as the sun went down. But by the 1970s we no longer needed to shop there because of the malls. And by the 1980s we no longer had to work there because of the now-you-see-it rise of industrial parks and office complexes. Pseudo-cities grew up, built of chrome, glass, and homogeneity. Half of America now lives in the 'burbs.

9. We abandoned America's cities.

10. Ronald Reagan and George Bush did, too, and so did many Democrats, truth be told. And they're going to have to ante up now. But it's not enough anymore to let those boys take all the responsibility. They don't carry it well enough.

11. I understand how Eugene Lang felt when he gave a speech at his old grade school, and, overwhelmed by the emptiness of words, offered all the students in the class a chance to go to college. I've heard the argument that Mr. Lang's **largesse** takes government off the hook. But I bet it's not compelling for kids who might have gone down the drain if one man hadn't remembered where he came from, before he moved on to someplace greener, richer, better.

12. Over the years I've heard about sister-city programs between places here and places abroad, places like Minsk or Vienna. Pen pals. Cultural exchange. Volunteer philanthropy. And all the while, twenty minutes away from the suburbs are cultures and lives and problems about which we are shamefully ignorant. I like the sister-city concept.

Short Hills and Newark. South-central L.A. and Simi Valley. Both sides benefit.

13. The pols will lose interest in the cities again soon enough, because so many city residents are poor and powerless and not white. It would be nice to think of Congress as the home of idealists, but thinking like that makes you feel awfully foolish. America's cities will prosper when America's prosperous citizens demand it. When they remember their roots.

14. I've walked many times down blocks like the one on which my father grew up. I've been a poverty tourist with a notebook, but I never felt ashamed of it until now.

15. On that little street were the ghosts of the people who brought me into being and the flesh-and-blood kids who will be my children's companions in the twenty-first century. You could tell by their eyes that they couldn't figure out why I was there. They were accustomed to being ignored, even by the people who had once populated their rooms. And as long as that continues, our cities will burst and burn, burst and burn, over and over again.

25. Which statement BEST explains the main idea of this essay?

　A. Many Americans are moving to the suburbs, causing serious problems in urban areas.

　B. The government must invest more in the people and property in urban areas.

　C. Americans have contributed to the problems of cities by abandoning the places of their roots.

　D. Both Republicans and Democrats are responsible for the plight of the cities.

26. Which of these details supports the main idea of the essay?

　A. Half of America now lives in the suburbs.

　B. Sister-city programs exist between places here and places abroad.

　C. It would be nice to think of Congress as the home of idealists, but thinking like that makes you feel foolish.

　D. The street on which the author's father grew up is a truncated little street that leads nowhere.

27. What does the writer of this essay want her readers to do?

   A. Support politicians who will take responsibility for urban conditions.

   B. Visit the cities more frequently to enjoy shopping and cultural activities.

   C. Talk to their relatives who once lived in urban areas to find out more about the past.

   D. Take some personal responsibility for improving living conditions in urban areas.

28. Ms. Quindlen admires Eugene Lang because

   A. he made a great deal of money even though he was poor when young.

   B. he made a generous offer to kids who attended his old elementary school.

   C. he still lives in his old neighborhood even though he could move to someplace better.

   D. he has been a champion of the sister-city programs for cities in the United States.

29. The author contrasts her father's street fifty years ago with the same street today to emphasize

   A. that many of the best things about cities have not changed over time.

   B. that her father's family suffered poverty and hardship over the years.

   C. that life was a lot easier in many ways in past generations.

   D. that the quality of life in city neighborhoods has seriously declined.

30. Which statement in the essay CANNOT be proven as true?

   A. The houses on the street are identical two-story attached brick buildings.

   B. Half of America now lives in the suburbs.

   C. America's cities will prosper when America's prosperous citizens demand it.

   D. I've walked many times down blocks like the one on which my father grew up.

31. In paragraph 8, what does the author suggest by her description of America's new "pseudo-cities"?

   A. America's new cities are bigger and better than the old ones.

   B. The new cities are artificial and uninteresting.

   C. The new cities will soon have many of the same problems as the old ones.

   D. The new cities are convenient places to work and shop.

32. What action would the author of this essay PROBABLY MOST support?

   A. exchange programs between urban schools and suburban schools

   B. clearing away run-down neighborhoods to build high-rise office towers and malls

C. relocating urban residents to new homes in the suburbs

D. the burning of decaying cities by angry residents

33. Which statement is a fact?

A. On that little street were the ghosts of the people who brought me into being.

B. This was a prosperous neighborhood, a way station to something better.

C. Twenty minutes away from the suburbs are cultures and lives and problems about which we are shamefully ignorant.

D. The small setback porch is still covered with debris from the fire that gutted the building several years ago.

34. What is the meaning of **largesse** in paragraph 11 of the essay?

A. emptiness

B. renewal

C. generosity

D. action

35. In Ms. Quindlen's version of the sister-city concept,

A. people would return to the cities to work and shop.

B. American cities and foreign cities would be linked.

C. cities and nearby suburbs would be linked in various ways.

D. politicians and citizens would work to rebuild cities.

36. What is the meaning of **synergy** in paragraph 8?

A. a clear answer

B. an obvious difficulty

C. a serious conflict

D. a working together

37. In paragraph 10, the author describes two Presidents and a number of Democratic lawmakers as "those boys." This choice of words is best described as

A. opinion.

B. a bandwagon appeal.

C. name-calling.

D. exaggeration.

38. In paragraph 12, the author claims, "Both sides benefit" from the sister-city program she imagines. In your own words, explain how both sides might benefit.

_____

_____

_____

39. Look at the author's choice of words in paragraphs 5, 6, 7, and 8. Find three or more examples of words with negative associations. Tell how the author uses this loaded language to help support her main idea.

_____

_____

_____

Read this recycling schedule for a suburban town. Then answer the questions that follow. Mark your answer choices on the answer sheet provided.

BOROUGH OF LAWNDALE RECYCLING SCHEDULE
Curbside Pickup Schedule

Month	Mon. Area A	Tues. Area E	Wed. Area C	Mon. Area B	Tues. Area F	Wed. Area D
January	5/19	6/20	7/21	12/26	13/27	14/28
February	2/19*	3/17	4/18	9/23	10/24	11/25
March	2/16/30	3/17/31	4/18	9/23	10/24	11/25
April	13/27	14/28	1/15/29	6/20	7/21	8/22
May	11/28*	12/26	13/27	4/18	5/19	6/20
June	8/22	9/23	10/24	1/15/29	2/16/30	3/17
July	6/20	7/21	8/22	13/27	14/28	1/15/29
August	3/17/31	4/18	5/19	10/24	11/25	12/26
September	14/28	1/15/29	2/16/30	10*/21	8/22	9/23
October	15*/26	13/27	14/28	5/19	6/20	7/21
November	9/23	10/24	11/25	2/16/30	3/17	4/18
December	7/21	8/22	9/23	14/28	1/15/29	2/16/30

Curbside pickup on holidays will be on the following Thursday.

STREET	AREA	STREET	AREA	STREET	AREA
Ackerson Rd.	B	Crescent Bend	A	Fox Run	B
Ada Pl.	D	Crescent Pl.	D	High St.	D
Albert Rd.	B	Dale Ave.	C	Hillside Ave.	
Allen St.	C	Delta Ct.	C	(#4-132)	C
Allison Village	A	De Mercurio Dr.	A	Hillside Ave	
Arcadia Rd.	B	Dogwood Dr.	F	(#149-585)	F
Bajor La.	B	Donnybrook Dr.	F	Homewood Ave.	A
Beatrice St.	D	Duffy Dr.	F	Hubbard Ct.	B
Beechwood Rd.	E	E. Allendale Ave.	A	Iroquois Ave.	B
Beresford Rd.	E	E. Crescent Ave.	B	Ivers Rd.	D
Berkshire Pl.	A	E. Elbrook Dr.	F	Kayeton Rd.	B
Bonnie Way	F	E. Orchard St.	A	Knolton Rd.	B
Boroline Rd.	A	Edgewood Rd.	E	Lake St.	C
Bradrick La.	E	Elbrook Dr.	F	Lakeview Dr.	B
Brookside Ave.		Elm St.	A	Lawrence La.	E
(#20-171)	C	Elmwood Ave.	A	Leigh Ct.	F
Brookside Ave		Erold Ct.	A	Linda Dr.	F
(#186-654)	E	Ethel Ave.	D	Lori La.	F
Burtwood Ct.	E	Fairhaven Dr.	F	Louise Ct.	A
Butternut Rd.	E	Farley Pl.	D	Surrey La.	F
Byron Ctr.	F	First St.	C	Talman Pl.	D
Cambridge Dr.	E	Forest Rd.	F	Thomas St.	C
Canaan Pl.	E	Fox Dr.	F	W. Crescent Ave.	D

HOLIDAY COLLECTION SCHEDULE

January 1, New Years Day	Thursday Collection (West Side) is on Friday 1/2. Friday Collection (East Side) is on Saturday 1/3.
May 25, Memorial Day	Monday Collection is on Tuesday 5/26. Tuesday Collection is on Wednesday 5/27. Wednesday Scrap Metal Collection is on Thursday 5/28. Thursday Collection is on Friday 5/29. Friday Collection is on Saturday 5/30.
July 4, 4th of July	All Collections are on regularly scheduled days.
September 7, Labor Day	Monday Collection is on Tuesday 9/8. Tuesday Collection is on Wednesday 9/9. Trash Collection (West Side) is on Thursday 9/10. Thursday Collection is on Friday 9/11. Friday Collection is on Saturday 9/12.
December 25, Christmas	Friday Collection is on Saturday 12/26.

Garbage collection only for the above holidays!
(Please refer to the Recycling Schedule for Holiday changes affecting Curbside Recycling Pickup.)

RULES AND REGULATIONS
Pertaining to Trash Collection
Borough Ordinance #747

Trash cannot be placed at the curb prior to 6:00 P.M. on the night preceding collection. All receptacles and any items not collected shall be removed by 6.00 P.M. on the day of said trash collection. Persons not doing so are liable to a summons and a penalty by fines of not less than $50.00 nor more than $500.00 per offense.

GUIDELINES FOR CURBSIDE PICKUP

- **GLASS:** Glass must be separated by color—clear, brown, green, and placed in separate containers. The maximum weight per container is 30 lbs. *Please rinse the container and remove and discard all tops and lids.*

- **ALUMINUM AND BI-METAL CANS:** All cans should be rinsed and clean of **debris**. Aluminum and Bi-Metal cans can be combined in one container.

- **PLASTICS:** All #1 (PETE) and #2 (HDPE) bottles are to be rinsed and clean of debris. Soda, milk, detergent, and bleach bottles are to be placed at the curb in either a large container or clear plastic bag. *Only #1 and #2 bottles can be recycled. Check for the recycling symbol on the bottom of the bottle. Caps should be removed.*

All of the above material can also be dropped off at the drop-off site.

- **CARDBOARD:** Cardboard must be flattened and tied with twine or heavy string. Cardboard must be placed at the curb by 7:00 A.M. on the 3rd Wednesday of each month or can be dropped off at the drop-off site.

- **SCRAP METAL:** (White Goods): Refrigerators, washers, dryers, cast iron radiators, etc. (any metal items), must be placed at the curb by 7:00 A.M. on the *4th Wednesday of each month.*

• NEWSPAPER COLLECTION

Newspapers must be tied with string or twine. Bundles shall be no larger than 12–15 inches high and no heavier than 25 lbs. *Only newspapers and their inserts will be collected.* All other materials found within the newspapers will be left at the curb. Newspapers will be collected on the following Saturdays by the Boy Scouts: 1/31, 3/21, 5/2, 6/13, 7/18, 8/22, 9/26, 11/7, 12/12.

• MAGAZINES, JUNK MAIL, AND OFFICE PAPER

Magazines, junk mail, and office paper is collected at the drop-off site at the compost area on W. Crescent Ave. All material must be placed in the appropriate containers. The drop-off site is open on Saturdays 9:00 A.M.–3:30 P.M. December 27 through March 28. Beginning on April 4th the drop-off site is open on Saturdays 9:00 A.M.–5:00 P.M. and Sundays 1:00 P.M.–5:00 P.M.

---

40. When does Area D get curbside pickup in November?

   A. the 4th and the 18th

   B. the 9th and the 23rd

   C. the 7th and the 21st

   D. the 5th and the 19th

41. Jason lives on Lawrence Lane. On which dates in July can he expect curbside pickup?

   A. the 9th and the 23rd

   B. the 10th and the 24th

   C. the 7th and the 21st

   D. the 5th and the 19th

42. When can residents expect a scrap metal collection during the week in which Memorial Day falls?

   A. 5/26

   B. 5/27

   C. 5/28

   D. 5/29

43. The Ramirezes missed the 6/13 newspaper collection and they will be away during all of July. When can they next put their newspapers out for collection?

   A. 7/3

   B. 8/18

   C. 8/22

   D. 9/26

44. Which street does NOT receive curbside pickup on Mondays?

   A. Arcadia Road

   B. Berkshire Place

   C. E. Orchard Street

   D. Dogwood Dr.

45. Mr. Haslup places his trash at curbside at 11:00 P.M. the night before a pickup. He retrieves his empty cans the next day after returning home from work at 7:00 P.M. What rule, if any, did he violate?

   A. He should have placed his garbage at the curb by 6 P.M. the night before.

   B. He should have waited until 6:00 A.M. of the morning of the pick-up day to bring his garbage outside.

   C. He should have brought his empty cans in by 6:00 P.M.

   D. Mr. Haslup violated no rule.

46. Old washing machines should be

   A. placed at the curb on the dates listed on the Recycling Schedule.

   B. placed at the curb on the 3rd Wednesday of each month.

C. placed at the curb on the 4th Wednesday of each month.

D. brought to the drop-off site on West Crescent Avenue only.

47. Which item placed outside for pick-up is NOT in accordance with borough regulations?

A. a clear plastic bag filled with both plastic milk and bleach containers

B. a 30-pound pile of newspapers tied with twine

C. a 30-pound container of clear glass bottles

D. a large pile of flattened cardboard tied with thick twine

48. Which items can be left at the curb or brought to the drop-off site?

A. glass

B. aluminum and bi-metal cans

C. plastic #1 and #2 bottles

D. all of the above

49. The drop-off site on West Crescent Avenue will NOT be open on

A. Saturday, December 27, at 9:00 A.M.

B. Saturday, March 28, at 4:00 P.M.

C. Saturday, April 4, at 4:00 P.M.

D. Sunday, April 5, at 2:00 P.M.

50. The trash collectors will make pickups along Delta Court on the same day they pick up on

A. Ada Place

B. Dogwood Drive

C. Fox Run

D. Lake Street

51. The meaning of **debris** is

A. labels, caps, and packaging materials.

B. the broken-down remains of something.

C. in accordance with stated rules.

D. any natural substance.

52. Based on the guidelines, it is MOST PROBABLE that

A. green and brown glass cannot be recycled.

B. plastics other than HDPE and PETE cannot be recycled.

C. most cardboard and newspaper is composted.

D. washers and dryers are rarely recycled.

53. Describe three possible problems that the Guidelines for Curbside Pickup are designed to prevent.

_____

_____

_____

Identifying Main Idea and Supporting Details

Most authors write in order to share ideas. Most of the information in the paragraph involves details that tell about, or support, the main idea. To understand a piece of writing, it's important to pay attention to the main ideas and supporting details.

Learn/ Review

The **main idea** of a paragraph is the most important point a writer makes. Sometimes the main idea of a pargraph is stated directly in a **topic sentence**. At other times, you have to determine the main idea from details in the passage. The sentences in a paragraph that tell about the main idea are called **supporting details**.

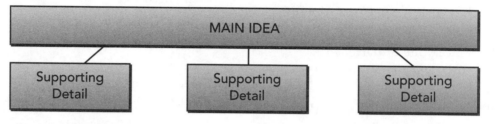

Practice/ Apply

Read this passage from a speech given by Chief Joseph of the Nez Percé as he surrendered to the United States Army in 1877. Then circle the letter of the correct answer to each question.

Tell General Howard I know his heart. What he told me before, I have in my heart. I am tired of fighting. Our chiefs are killed; Looking Glass is dead, Ta-Hool-Hool-Shute is dead. The old men are all dead. It is the young men who say yes or no. He who led on the young men is dead. It is cold, and we have no blankets; the little children are freezing to death. My people, some of them, have run away to the hills, and have no blankets, no food. No one knows where they are—perhaps freezing to death. I want to have time to look for my children, and see how many I can find. Maybe I shall find them among the dead. Hear me, my chiefs! I am tired; my heart is sick and sad. From where the sun now stands I will fight no more forever.

1. What is the main idea of this paragraph?
   A. The chief's people are freezing in the cold winter weather.
   B. The important chiefs of the tribe have been killed.
   C. Chief Joseph's children have been killed in battle.
   D. Chief Joseph will no longer fight against the United States Army.

2. Which detail does Chief Joseph give to support his main idea?
   A. General Howard has begged him to surrender.
   B. Many of his people have been moved to a reservation.
   C. He is tired of the fighting and wants to save his remaining people.
   D. The old men of the tribe have advised him to seek peace.

Mini-Lesson 2 | Recognizing Cause and Effect

Why are some species endangered? Why wasn't the governor reelected to a second term? Why do hurricanes strike with such force? Writers often focus on why things happen. Looking for the reasons things happen will help you understand the events you read about.

Learn/ Review

When one thing causes something else to happen, the process is called **cause and effect**. A **cause** is an event that makes something happen. An **effect** is what happens. As the chart below shows, an effect may have several causes. Similarly, a cause may have several effects.

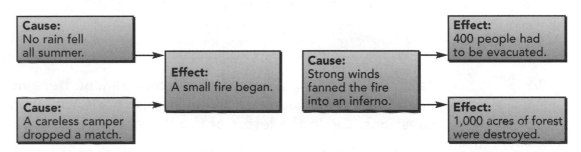

Practice/ Apply

Read the following passage and look for examples of cause and effect. Circle the letter of the correct answer to each question.

It is the first of February, and everyone is talking about starlings. Starlings came to this country on a passenger liner from Europe. One hundred of them were deliberately released in Central Park, and from those hundred descended all of our countless millions of starlings today. According to Edwin Way Teale, "Their coming was the result of one man's fancy. That man was Eugene Schieffelin, a wealthy New York drug manufacturer. His curious hobby was the introduction into America of all the birds mentioned in William Shakespeare." The birds adapted to their new country splendidly.

—Annie Dillard, *Pilgrim at Tinker Creek*

1. Why did Eugene Schieffelin cause starlings to be imported to America?

   A. He knew that they would adapt splendidly to conditions here.

   B. He liked seeing the birds in Central Park.

   C. Passengers on ocean liners enjoyed having the birds on board.

   D. He wanted all of the birds mentioned in Shakespeare to be in America.

2. As a result of Schieffelin's actions,

   A. everyone now talks about starlings every February.

   B. all the birds mentioned by Shakespeare are now in America.

   C. untold millions of starlings now live in the United States.

   D. many other non-native birds have been released in the United States.

Mini-Lesson 3 | Making Inferences

Suppose you were to see your upstairs neighbors buying cat food at the store, even though your apartment building had a "No Pets" policy. You hear the scampering of tiny feet above you at night, and your sister, who's allergic to cats, is sneezing a lot all of a sudden. Based on these details, you might infer that your neighbor has gotten a cat.

**Learn/
Review**

You make **inferences** when you read, too. Writers don't tell you everything. They expect you to read between the lines and fill in some information for yourself. To make an inference, you combine the clues in a piece of writing with what you already know.

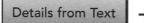

| Details from Text | + | Your Own Knowledge | → | Inference |

**Practice/
Apply**

Read the following passage about chimpanzee behavior. Then use clues from the passage and your own experience to answer the questions. Circle the letter of the correct answer to each question.

In addition, chimpanzees communicate by touch or gesture. A mother touches her young one when she is about to move away, or taps on the trunk when she wants it to come down from a tree. When a chimpanzee is anxious for a share of some delicacy, he begs, holding out his hand palm up, exactly as we do. He may pat the branch beside him if he wants a companion to join him there. When two animals are grooming each other and one feels that it is his turn to be groomed, he often reaches out and gives his companion a poke.

Once, when three males were all grooming one another, I saw a female going round poking at each of them in turn. But she was completely ignored—and so sat down sadly and groomed herself!

There are also many gestures of greeting and friendship. Sometimes when two friends meet after a separation, they fling their arms around each other in a delighted embrace.

—Jane Goodall, *From the Field*

1. From the details and what you know from real life, you might infer that
   A. male chimpanzees are better groomed than females.
   B. chimps prefer to be groomed by others rather than grooming themselves.
   C. chimpanzees spend most of the day grooming their fur.
   D. chimpanzees only groom their parents or siblings.

2. You can also infer from details in the passage that
   A. mother chimpanzees allow their children a great deal of freedom to roam.
   B. chimpanzees would not be able to learn to use spoken language.
   C. chimpanzees are very generous about sharing their food with one another.
   D. some chimpanzees have strong feelings for one another.

Recognizing Sequence

You use calendars to keep track of the days and months. You have daily schedules to follow, and you check your watches to keep track of the time. Time sequence, the order in which things happen, is the main way in which everyone organizes his or her life.

**Learn/
Review**

Sequence is a way to organize the events in stories and articles. Being aware of the sequence of events can help you better understand the stories and articles you read. Writers sometimes use time clue words, such as *first, next, then, later,* and *finally* to show sequence. You can use a chart like this to list the sequence of events in a story or passage.

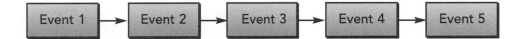

**Practice/
Apply**

As you read this passage, think about the sequence of events. Then circle the letter of the correct answer to each question.

Surprisingly, the very first Chinese to set foot on United States soil were not adventurers or laborers in search of gold but students in search of knowledge. In 1847, a year before the glitter of that metallic substance caught the eye of John Marshall on the south bank of the American River, an American missionary, the Reverend S. R. Brown, had brought with him three Chinese boys to the United States to study at the Monson Academy in Massachusetts. One of them was Yung Wing, who later graduated from Yale and who attained high office in the Chinese government. He was successful in persuading the Emperor to send other students to the United States for specialized training and education, almost all of whom eventually rendered distinguished service to their country, then emerging from her self-isolation.

—Betty Lee Sung, *Mountain of Gold: The Story of the Chinese in America*

1. The first Chinese came to America
   A. long before gold was discovered in California.
   B. shortly before gold was discovered in California.
   C. the same year gold was discovered in California.
   D. shortly after gold was discovered in California.

2. Yung Wing studied at Yale
   A. after attaining high office in the Chinese government.
   B. while persuading the Emperor to send students to the United States.
   C. when China was emerging from her self-isolation.
   D. after coming to the United States as a boy.

Comparing and Contrasting

Comparing and contrasting is a way to "size up" the world. Whether you're choosing a movie, a restaurant, or a CD to buy, you're likely to compare and contrast a few possibilities before making your decision.

When you notice how things are alike, you are **comparing**. When you notice how things are different, you are **contrasting**.

A Venn diagram is one way to show how two things are alike and different. This Venn diagram compares and contrasts some features of alligators and crocodiles.

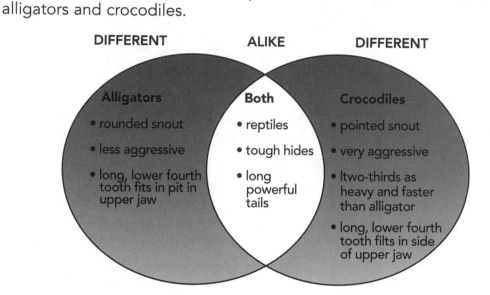

DIFFERENT   ALIKE   DIFFERENT

Alligators
- rounded snout
- less aggressive
- long, lower fourth tooth fits in pit in upper jaw

Both
- reptiles
- tough hides
- long powerful tails

Crocodiles
- pointed snout
- very aggressive
- two-thirds as heavy and faster than alligator
- long, lower fourth tooth fits in side of upper jaw

As you read the passage, think about how the two types of drums are alike and different. Then circle the letter of the correct answer.

Back in the 1940s, musicians in the West Indies used old oil barrels to create a completely new instrument—steel drums. Like the band drums used in popular music, steel drums are percussion instruments. Both require a musician with a good sense of rhythm to beat the drumhead with drumsticks. That's where the similarities stop, however. Band drums usually have plastic drumheads, while a steel drum musician beats on the steel bottom of a barrel. The steel drumhead has been hammered and heated in special ways, so that each section produces a different musical note. Band drums, by contrast, do not produce musical notes, only a single tone.

1. Both steel drums and band drums
   A. have plastic drumheads.
   B. produce musical notes.
   C. are played with drumsticks.
   D. are hammered and heated to produce certain tones.

2. Unlike steel drums, band drums
   A. require a musician with a good sense of rhythm.
   B. produce a single tone.
   C. were created in the West Indies.
   D. are a percussion instrument.

Classifying

Why is the men's clothing section on one floor of a department store, housewares on another floor, and sporting goods on a third? Why does the library keep all the biographies in one section and the fiction in another?

Classifying is grouping items together that have something in common. It's a way to select and organize details conveniently and logically. Often you form **categories**, or groups, when you classify. Chances are you classify objects into categories when you put away your clothes, your tools, or your groceries.

Category 1	Category 2

As you read the following passage, think about the categories of Victorian architecture. Then circle the letter of the correct answer.

Victorian is too general a term to describe a building since many styles of architecture were popular in the Victorian era. The Italianate style, for example, was widespread in the United States from 1850 to 1900. Modeled after Renaissance architecture in Italy, an Italianate house has an overhanging roof decorated with curved brackets. The doors and windows feature ornamental caps or arches. By the mid-1800s, the Gothic Revival style had also gained influence here. Like medieval churches, Gothic Revival buildings have pointed, arched windows and ornate gables. Another Victorian style, the Romanesque Revival, added solidity and dignity to public buildings built after the Civil War. Usually brick, a Romanesque structure has heavy, round forms and bold decorations around windows and doorways. When it comes to Victorian houses, however, Queen Anne is the style that most often comes to mind. Queen Anne houses have asymmetrical floor plans, and their elaborate chimneys and towers create a fanciful outline. Porches, balconies and fancy shinglework add to the impact.

1. A Victorian house in the Italianate style would have
   A. pointed, arched windows.
   B. elaborate chimneys.
   C. bold decorations around the windows.
   D. an overhanging roof with decorative brackets.

2. If you saw a solid-looking courthouse with heavy, round walls and decorated brickwork, it would PROBABLY be an example of
   A. the Italianate style.
   B. the Gothic Revival style.
   C. the Romanesque Revival style.
   D. the Queen Anne style.

Distinguishing Fact and Opinion

Which of these statements could you prove to be true?

- Harriet Tubman was born a slave in Maryland, one of eleven sons and daughters.

- Harriet Tubman led a charmed life.

Learn/ Review

A **fact** is a statement known to be true, something that can be checked or proven. You could check the facts about Harriet Tubman's birth and family in a biography or in historical records. An **opinion** is a statement that expresses a personal judgment, feeling, or belief. Opinions cannot be checked and proven to be true. You might agree or disagree with the opinion that Tubman led a charmed life, but there is no way to prove that she did.

Practice/ Apply

Read this passage and think about which statements are facts and which are opinions. Then circle the letter of the correct answer.

Harriet Tubman became known as a "conductor" on the Underground Railroad. She was not the only "conductor" but she was the most famous, and one of the most daring. Once she brought as many as twenty-five slaves in a single band to freedom . . . . within twelve years she made nineteen dangerous trips into the South rescuing slaves.

She might have been a great actress . . . . without makeup she could hollow out her cheeks and wrinkle her brow to seem like a very old woman. She would make her body shrink and cause her legs to totter when she chose to disguise herself.

Harriet Tubman's war activities were amazing. She served under General Stevens at Beaufort, South Carolina. She was sent to Florida to nurse those ill of dysentery, smallpox, and yellow fever. She was with Colonel Robert Gould Shaw at Fort Wagner. She organized a group of nine Negro scouts and river pilots, and, with Colonel Montgomery, led a Union raiding contingent of three gunboats and about 150 Negro troops up the Combahee River.

—Langston Hughes, *Famous American Negroes*

1. Which statement is a fact?
   A. Harriet Tubman's war activities were amazing.
   B. She was with Colonel Robert Gould Shaw at Fort Wagner.
   C. She was the most famous conductor, and one of the most daring.
   D. She might have been a great actress.

2. Which statement is an opinion?
   A. She brought twenty-five slaves in a single band to freedom.
   B. She served under General Stevens at Beaufort, South Carolina.
   C. Harriet Tubman's war activities were amazing.
   D. She led a Union raiding contingent up the Combahee River.

Making Generalizations

Suppose two of your friends took up jogging, lost weight, and stayed slim. Two other friends dieted, lost weight, but then regained it. Based on this, you might say: *Joggers tend to lose weight permanently more than dieters.* Although you might not realize it, you would have made a generalization.

Learn/
Review

A **generalization** is a rule or statement that applies to many different situations or events. To make a generalization, you take information you read about in a text and apply the information in a broader sense. One generalization might be: *Retrievers usually make excellent dogs for families with children.* Generalizations often contain signal words such as *in general, usually, few, tend to,* or *most.*

Practice/
Apply

Read the following passage about radon gas. Then circle the letter of the correct answer to each question.

Radon is a naturally occurring radioactive gas formed by the decay of uranium in rock. Colorless and odorless, radon gas seeps into houses through cracks in the foundation. If the surrounding soil contains a great deal of radon, more of the gas is likely to enter a house. In a well-insulated house, radon tends to build up. As radon gas decays, its by-products may be trapped in the lungs where they release radiation. Even a little radiation can damage lung tissue, and even a little lung tissue damage can lead many years later to lung cancer. The EPA estimates that 5,000 to 20,000 lung cancer deaths every year are caused by radon, although some scientists say this is too high. (About 110,000 annual lung cancer deaths are due to smoking.) Every house has some radon, and special radon detectors are needed to measure the gas. If the radon level in a house is above safe levels, it's important to reduce the danger. Sealing a house foundation prevents the gas from entering while installing basement fans moves the radon out.

1. Which of these statements is supported by information in the paragraph?
   A. Anything taken in excess will cause some kind of cancer.
   B. It is possible to eliminate the source of radon gas from the soil.
   C. Scientists disagree about how much lung cancer is caused by radon.
   D. Often, we are unaware of environmental dangers.

2. Based on the information in this passage, you can generalize that
   A. some cancers are caused by factors that affected us years ago.
   B. there is little we can do to limit or resolve a radon problem.
   C. radon detectors can be a lifesaver in some areas of the country.
   D. radon gas causes much more lung cancer than smoking.

Using Context Clues

As you read more and more, your vocabulary gradually grows. That's partly because you learn to use clues in a reading passage to figure out the meaning of the new words you come across.

Learn/ Review

The **context** is the sentence or passage in which a word appears. Any details in the context that provide hints to the meaning of a word are **context clues**. Here are the six common types of context clues:

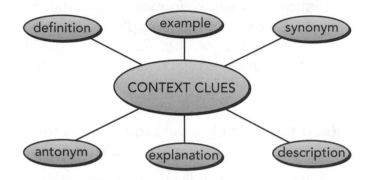

- Sometimes the context clues in a sentence are a **definition** of a new or unfamiliar word.

  Early Carolina farmers built *plantations*, <u>large farms that grow one main cash crop.</u>

- A writer might also clear up a word's meaning by giving an **example**.

  The patient suffered serious *trauma* in the accident; <u>she had a fractured skull, a broken leg, and internal bleeding.</u>

- Often, the context has a word that is a **synonym** for an unfamiliar word.

  The applause reached a deafening *crescendo*; after this <u>high point,</u> however, the audience quickly exited the hall.

- An **antonym** can also serve as a context clue to a word's meaning.

  Thirty years ago the school had a *deplorable* reputation; fortunately, that's all changed, and now the institution gets <u>top-notch</u> ratings.

- An **explanation** will often clear up the meaning of the word.

  The merchant provided the prospector with <u>equipment and money;</u> in return for this *grubstake*, he would receive <u>10 percent of any gold the miner discovered.</u>

- **Descriptions** also contain details that serve as context clues.

  The first *harquebus* was so <u>heavy that a knight had to place it in a special support before firing it.</u>

Read each passage. Then circle the letter of the correct answer.

Another cause of World War I was the **arms race** that had developed in Europe. An arms race is a rivalry among nations to gain the greatest military power. Most countries developed **munitions** industries to produce guns and cannons. Stand-by armies were established, and only in case of trouble would these **reserve** forces be mobilized. The European nations hoped their new weapons and trained soldiers would **forestall** the likelihood of war. Instead, however, the heightened military readiness almost seemed to provoke open conflict.

1. Which type of context clue gives you the meaning of **arms race**?
   A. example
   B. definition
   C. antonym
   D. description

2. What is the meaning of **munitions**?
   A. heavy machinery
   B. high-tech equipment
   C. weapons
   D. foodstuffs

3. In this passage, **reserve** means
   A. a tract of public land set apart.
   B. caution in words and actions.
   C. a military group held back from action.
   D. gold or other funds kept on hand to meet expenses.

4. What does **forestall** mean?
   A. increase
   B. prevent
   C. draw out
   D. popularize

In August of 1914, the well-trained German army conquered Belgium in just three weeks. After this successful **blitzkrieg**, the Germans quickly moved into France where their armies experienced less **propitious** results. French and British armies stopped the Germans at the Marne River in September. At that point, the fighting reached a stalemate, meaning that neither side was able to advance. Instead the opponents dug a line of trenches that stretched nearly 300 miles from the Belgian coast to Switzerland. For over three years, a bloody war of **attrition** was waged in which both sides suffered many casualties without gaining much territory.

5. Which type of context clue gives you the meaning of **blitzkrieg**?
   A. example
   B. definition
   C. antonym
   D. description

6. In this passage, **propitious** means
   A. unfavorable.
   B. favorable.
   C. fast.
   D. well-trained.

7. A war of **attrition** is
   A. fast and successful.
   B. long and costly.
   C. without a decisive end.
   D. fought with modern munitions.

GLOSSARY

antonyms: words with opposite meanings

bandwagon appeal: a technique that persuades the reader or listener to do something by emphasizing that a great many others are doing so

categories: groups of items that have something in common

cause: an event that makes something happen

central purpose: the focus of an informational text; what the author most wants you to learn by reading the text

characters: the people in a short story or novel

character traits: the qualities of a character that a reader discovers as a story unfolds

classify: to organize information into categories

compare: to show ways in which two or more things are similar

conflict: a struggle between two or more opposing forces

context: the sentence or passage in which a word appears

context clues: details in the context that provide hints to a word's meaning

contrast: to show ways in which two or more things differ

effect: the result of a cause

encyclopedia index: a list of references to each topic in the volumes of an encyclopedia

everyday text: a type of writing you see in everyday situations

exaggeration: a statement that enlarges something beyond the truth

fact: a statement known to be true or one that can be checked or proven

figures of speech: the use of imaginative language that is not meant to be taken as a literal truth

generalization: a rule or statement that applies to many different situations

hyperbole: a figure of speech that creates a striking image by exaggerating something

index: an alphabetical list of terms or topics in a book and the pages on which they are mentioned

infer: to combine details from the text with your own personal knowledge to reach a logical conclusion

informational text: writing that mainly gives information about a topic

loaded language: a persuasive technique that takes advantage of the strong positive or negative feelings that people associate with certain words

major idea: the most important idea in a paragraph or passage of text

metaphor: a figure of speech that makes a comparison by stating that one thing is another

mood: the general atmosphere of a narrative

motivation: a feeling or goal that causes a character to act in a certain way

name-calling: a persuasive technique that labels someone or something in a negative way

narrative text: writing that tells a story

opinion: a statement expressing a personal belief, feeling, or judgment; one that cannot be checked or proven

personification: a figure of speech that gives human traits or abilities to an animal or object

persuasive techniques: methods used to persuade readers

persuasive text: writing that tries to influence the reader to act or think in a certain way

plot: the sequence of events that happens in a story or novel

problem: a difficulty or conflict that a character faces in a story

resolution: the part of a story plot in which a conflict is resolved

sequence: the order in which things happen in a story

setting: the time and place in which the action of a story takes place

simile: a figure of speech that makes a comparison between two things using *like* or *as*

supporting details: details that develop and explain the major or main ideas

synonyms: words with the same or similar meanings

synthesize: to combine the information from one or more texts to make a decision or reach a conclusion

table of contents: a list of chapters or other parts of a book and the pages on which they begin

theme: the main idea or message that an author wants the reader to think about

timeline: a visual aid that divides a period of time into segments and lists important events

topic sentence: the sentence that states the main idea of a paragraph

visual aids: graphs, maps, tables, and timelines that organize a great deal of information in an easy-to-use form